Those Other Religions In Your Neighborhood

Those Other Religions In Your Neighborhood

Loving your neighbor when you don't know how

TERRY C. MUCK

ZondervanPublishingHouse
Academic and Professional Books
Grand Rapids, Michigan
A Division of HarperCollins*Publishers*

Those Other Religions in Your Neighborhood

Requests for information should be addressed to:
Zondervan Publishing House
Academic and Professional Books
Grand Rapids, Michigan 49530

Library of Congress Cataloging-in-Publication Data

Muck, Terry C., 1947-
Those other religions in your neighborhood: loving your neighbor when you don't know how / Terry C. Muck.
p. cm.
Includes bibliographical references.
ISBN 0-310-54041-0
1. United States–Religion–1960- 2. Religious pluralism–United States–History–20th century. 3. Evangelistic work–United States. 4. Witness bearing (Christianity). 5. Neighborliness–Religious aspects–Christianity. I. Title.
BL2525.M85 1992
261.2'0973–dc20 92-14188
CIP

Edited by Leonard G. Goss and Laura Weller
Cover design by Jack Foster
Cover illustration by Corey Wilkinson

Printed in the United States of America

92 93 94 95 96 97 / CH / 10 9 8 7 6 5 4 3 2 1

To my students at
Austin Presbyterian Theological Seminary—
especially Amy, Clarence, David, Ginny,
Greg, Jack, James, Karen, Pat, Peggy,
Sharyn, and Sue—who helped focus the questions
and looked for examples.

Contents

Part 3
Sharing Faith

Introduction

THE GROWTH OF NON-CHRISTIAN RELIGIONS IN THE United States has been one of my primary interests for many years. In large part, my interest has been scholarly. My graduate degrees are in comparative religion, so the study of the increasingly plural religious mix of America is a natural extension of my scholarly work in Buddhism, Hinduism, and Islam.

My interest, however, goes beyond the scholarly; it grows also out of a more personal, theological interest. To put it simply, I do not think that American Christians are properly prepared for religious competition.

My use of the term *religious competition* is a dead giveaway to how I will be describing the challenge of non-Christian religions on American turf. Christianity *is* competing with the other world religions, but do not jump to conclusions about what that means. Most of this book describes the form I think this new competition should take, so it is premature to describe it in detail here.

However, I will say that I use the word *competition,* in part, to startle you. We Christians have been an uncontested majority in this country for so long that it is difficult to think of other religions challenging us here—in Chicago, Cedar Rapids, Lincoln, Austin, and Helena. This is, after all, America, founded on Christian principles by Northern European Protestants. We used to think of religious pluralism as the tiffs that Episcopalians, Congregationalists, and Presbyterians got into over how to run their churches. The addition of Roman Catholicism to that mix was almost too much to bear.

Now Christian denominationalism is the least of our worries. The religious marketplace has become very crowded. One in ten Americans claims to belong to a non-Christian religion. And, to say it again, I do not think that we are ready for the competition.

It is time to get ready, especially on the most basic level of all, the neighborhood level. Last spring, my thirteen-year-old son was invited to religious services of his two best friends. One was a bar mitzvah, a Jewish adulthood initiation ceremony; the other was a Hindu Vedic initiation ceremony (*upanayana*) for thirteen-year-old Amitav. For my wife, Judy, and I the question of religious pluralism suddenly became more than an academic exercise. We had to decide whether David should go to these services. That meant that we needed good reasons, both for our decision and for an explanation to David. (See chapter 7 for how Judy and I handled David's experience.)

In scores of small, almost imperceptible ways, religious competition is taking place on the neighborhood level. Children playing, men and women talking, households living out everyday activities—the different levels of interaction are endless.

Usually when we think of interaction with people of other religious traditions, we think of conversion. For many of us, the worst-case scenario would be for one of our children to be converted to another religion or, worse, a cult. In chapter 6 I tell the story of Arthur Brown, whose son Tom started a spiritual search during his college years that currently has him in India studying with a Hindu guru. With the growing number of other religions in our country, this type of scenario will probably increase in frequency.

Another kind of conversion will increase in frequency. For many of us, the best-case scenario would be for someone of another religious tradition to convert to Christianity. A good friend of mine, Ron Itano, was a Japanese Buddhist who found Christ while watching an American televangelist present the Gospel. Interreligious interaction often leads to change.

The truth of interreligious interaction, however, is far different from either one of these scenarios. Conversions do take place—in both directions. But when compared with the tens of thousands of informal, everyday, seemingly inconsequential contacts American Christians make with members of other religious traditions, conversions (either way) are very small in number.

Yet these less dramatic contacts do produce questions. Questions about lifestyle, permissible and impermissible exchanges of ideas, the wisdom of friendships over against more formal relationships—these and scores of other questions crowd the docket of everyday experience.

This book is largely about contacts that do not feature immediate conversion, although we do discuss the question of conversion in chapter 9. It is about life in the neighborhoods where you and I live. It is there, in the neighborhoods and not in academia, that religious pluralism is having its greatest impact. And it is in the small, everyday decisions about what kind of contact we want to have with Hindu, Buddhist, Muslim, Mormon, New Age, and Native American neighbors that the theological die is being cast that will shape the future of the American Christian church.

In short, the questions in the following chapters are everyday in format, but they are eternal in implication.

1
The Religions Are Coming

"IT'S CHAOS," THE FRUSTRATED TEACHER SAID. "When I grew up it was calm and peaceful. We started the school day with prayer, then pledged allegiance to the flag, and then the teacher read a verse or two from the Bible. Now we don't do any of that. Wouldn't dare. Some of the kids are from India—Hindus mostly. Others are from the Middle East—Muslims. It's chaos to get them all to follow along on the same page long enough to do schoolwork. So many different kinds of children, so little common ground."

The speaker was a female public school teacher in a mid-sized Texas town. The outburst of emotion came during an Episcopalian Sunday school class I was teaching on religious pluralism in America. She was not really angry, just frustrated. The many different religions represented by the students in her class were causing her some very practical problems. Her teaching was hampered, and she wanted help.

Another man in a Baptist church wanted to know if it was true that when a Muslim soldier was killed by an infidel, the soldier went straight to heaven. A young woman in that same class wanted to know if her two Buddhist girlfriends from college were really going to hell. A mother asked if she should allow her two young children to play with Indian children from the Hindu temple in their neighborhood. They all wanted answers.

The rapidly growing phenomenon of world religions in our midst has raised a host of such practical questions. Americans generally are beyond the stage of wondering if religious pluralism is here to stay. "It's not going to go away," noted a retired banker in a Presbyterian church. "Like it or not, the religions are with us. We need to figure out what to do about it."

The retired banker is right that the religions are here to stay. In the United States there are more Muslims than Presbyterians, more Buddhists than Assembly of God members, and almost as many Hindus as Episcopalians. Immigration patterns, birthrates, conversion statistics, and intellectual trends insure that this growth of non-Christian religions will continue.

Scholars call this diversity of religions in America *religious pluralism*, but different scholars mean different things by the term. Some use it simply as a description of the way things are: this is called *de facto pluralism*, the fact of pluralism. This is the way we will use the term in this book.

Others use the term in a more technical sense, what one might call *philosophical pluralism*. When used this way, pluralism describes a position that says that a variety of religious traditions should be the norm. That is, human beings were meant to have a rich diversity of religious beliefs, and the best way to approach this diversity is as a good and healthy situation. Since no one religious tradition can possibly be true to the exclusion of others, let us just say that all religions describe truth in their own way. In a very real sense, this approach to religious pluralism is as great a challenge to Christians as is the fact of non-Christian religions.

I say this because, at the same time that non-Christian religions are growing in this country, many Christian denominations are in rapid decline. Although some smaller denominations and independent churches still project growth, the largest groups have shown steady erosion of members, and several face either extinction, radical cutbacks in ministry, or fragmentation due to squabbles in their ranks—an in-house version of the same religious pluralism we see between religions and between denominations.

Ironically, much of this in-house fighting centers around how to deal with the pluralism they see in society at large! One has only to sit on a denominational task force, as I have, and listen to the extraordinary variety of theological positions within Christian denominations to know that pluralism is almost as big a problem within the church as without it.

In the meantime, church members face a number of practical problems about relationships with those from other religions. They want theologically sound, scripturally based answers, of course. But the problems are in the real world—here-and-now problems that do not succumb to easy answers.

Important religious questions usually do not have easy answers. The questions people are asking in Sunday school classes are practical and down to earth, as we have seen. However, in attempting solid answers to them, we are quickly led to the most important questions of life: Who am I? What am I doing here? Where am I going? Those questions, in turn, lead to the core doctrines of the Christian faith regarding creation, revelation, and salvation.

There is one more complicating factor: theologians, even card-carrying conservative ones, do not agree on the answers. I took a personal survey of three of the conservative theologians I admire most, scholars whose names you would immediately recognize as the shapers of our theological thought today. I asked them, "What does the growing religious pluralism of our day mean for conservative theology?"

One said, "We must not change a thing. We must simply stay the course and preach the Gospel." The second said, "We must go back to our basic theology [of the Reformers] and reeducate our people to think theologically. If they knew how to think theologically, none of this would be a problem." The third said, "We must accept the theological challenge and show how the Gospel speaks to the pluralistic cultural climate of the day."

Although there is certainly truth in what each of these scholars says, they obviously do not agree on what should be the focus of our theological task. If they cannot agree on fundamental strategy, what hope is there for laypersons who face the challenge of the religions in their own neighborhoods? Perhaps a good place to start is to understand how we got into this condition of radical pluralism.

Pluralism in America

As Christians everywhere become more and more aware of the religious pluralism around them, the demand for answers increases. In the past year I have taught more than thirty Sunday school classes on this subject, and there have been some in every class who had no idea about the growth of non-Christian religions in America or adopted the position that "it can't happen here."

I have learned an effective way to impress Sunday school students with the here-and-now-ness of religious pluralism. Before the class, I find the phone book for that particular town, turn to the yellow-page listing of churches, and jot down the non-Christian churches, temples, mosques, and meeting halls in that town. The list has never been short, and the impact has never failed to be convincing.

There are non-Christian religious groups everywhere in America. Gordon Melton, editor of *The Encyclopedia of American Religions*, notes that there are more than 1,500 religious groups in America today, and more than 600 of them are non-Christian. Some of those groups, particularly those representing the historic world religions, are large. As I detail in my book *Alien Gods on American Turf,*[1] Hindus, Buddhists, and Muslims have significant, large populations in America today, larger than many of our historic Protestant denominations. Other non-Christian groups number in the millions also, particularly those with Christian roots that have become unorthodox, such as Mormons, Christian Science, and Jehovah's Witnesses. Most of the 600 non-Christian groups are smaller "new religions" and cults, but even those add up to a sizable number of people. A recent Gallup poll indicates a growing number of people who claim to be in the category of "other religion," a category that used to be about 2 to 3 percent of the population but now is approaching 10 percent.

Estimating the size of religious groups in the United States has always been a chancy affair. Since official government census takers are not allowed to ask religious affiliation questions, we are forced to rely on self-reporting by religious groups (figures susceptible to the "evangelistically-speaking" syndrome) and poll-taking firms. If, however, we accept Gallup's figures and match them with the 1990 census figures, we find that 10 percent of 175 million, the approximate size of the United States adult population, means that 17.5 million people in the United States claim a non-Christian religion as their own.

Even my skeptical Sunday school class members begin to sit up and take notice when the figures exceed ten million. Yet I always feel it necessary to jar them just a bit further out of their complacency. It is too easy to see these groups of people as statistics—inert masses around which we can move and work with little contact or effect. But these are active people, more often than not gaining in political, cultural, and economic influence, and often doing aggressive missionary work of their own.

A recent article in the *New York Times* illustrates the potential influence of these groups.[2] Asian-American students are capturing more and more of the academic prizes our educational institutions have to offer. Although Asian-Americans comprise just 2.8 percent of our general population, Asian-American students make up 12 percent of Harvard's population, 20 percent of Stanford's, and 30 percent of Berkeley's. Researchers like UCLA psychologist Stanley Sue, the article reported, suspect that a drive to escape discrimination is one of the prime motivators (along with just plain hard work) explaining this trend.

Can that same drive be prompting these students, many of whom are Buddhist (and some other immigrant groups representing Hindus and Muslims), to promote their religions here in the United States? The evidence that they are doing so is everywhere. Japanese Buddhism in particular is growing significantly among American blacks and young people. The Naropa Institute in Boulder, Colorado, is a fully accredited four-year liberal arts college with a good academic reputation. It was founded by Tibetan Buddhists who administer its programs today. Hindus have temples in every major city, run summer camps in Hindu teachings for young people, and publish a fine newspaper, *Hinduism Today*, with a circulation of 180,000. The most aggressive evangelizers, however, are the Muslims, who already have a strong base in the American black community and are now reaching out to white, suburban audiences. Every town of any size in the United States has a mosque, a Muslim place of worship. Check the phone book.

The religions *are* coming, and they are going to make a difference in every aspect of our lives, whether we like it or not.

The Roots of Pluralism

Immigration accounts for the physical presence of many non-Christian religious groups. Elsewhere I have shown how the major groups came to be a part of our cultural scene.[3] But more is at work here than physical presence. An intellectual and social shift is accentuating the pluralistic climate. The most recent social phenomena that brought this shift to light were the new religious movements of the sixties. However, the sixties are better seen as the end result of a long process.

The intellectual shift really has its roots in the European Enlightenment, which led to all the -isms we hear about ad nauseam in social commentary and sermons, such as rationalism, scientism, and secularism. In the past two hundred years, the Christian religion has lost its pride of place as culture's dominant intellectual authority. Before that, whenever there was an important philosophical question that Western civilization needed answered, the Christian theologians were the ones who answered it. But the Enlightenment changed that. At first the secular intellectuals took the theologian's place and then, particularly in America, the scientists took over. Predictably, the answers provided by both the humanist intellectuals and the scientists have not worked.

For example, existentialism was supposed to explain and help us cope with the growing anxiety of modern living, but the signs of uncontrollable anxiety—loneliness, despair, and depression—have reached epidemic proportions in spite of existentialist explanations.

Or take another example, this one from science. The theory of evolution was supposed to explain both human origins and human destiny, but even scientific evolutionists cannot agree on either one, and the questions of origins for biologists, astronomers, and mathematicians are murkier than ever.

By the time we began to see, about twenty years ago, that the intellectuals and scientists could not handle the job we had trustingly given them (most scientists, at least, did not want it in the first place), it was too late to go back to the theologians. Most of them had either decided to imitate the intellectuals, becoming little more than humanist philosophers in the process, or else managers, social workers, and therapists. It is just as well. The world had changed so drastically in the interim that the way the theologian's answers used to be implemented, through authoritative, hierarchical church structures, would no longer work. People no longer learned through dictated theological argument. People now learn through personal experience and do-it-yourself theology, and not just from one institutional authority but from scores of ad hoc "institutions." Personal freedom and institutional diversity have made the modern world a very different place to be. Churches do not make religious people;

rather, religious people make churches—all kinds of custom-made "churches."

When people talk about the challenge of modern pluralism, they are talking about a culture where authority is diffused and individual freedom runs rampant.

How Do Christians Answer the Challenge of Pluralism?

The Christian's task can be summed up succinctly, no matter what the cultural setting. The challenge, as Paul phrased it in Ephesians 4:15, is to speak the truth in love. Speak the truth and love your neighbor. Both are clear teachings of Scripture, and because of their fundamental status in Christian theology, they have almost become cliches.

The danger of cliches, of course, is that we forget what they really mean even as we mouth them with undying endorsement. If you have any doubt about what these phrases mean, or if you want to follow the tracks of their teaching in the Bible, see the appendix at the back of this book. For now, however, let us assume we know what we mean when we say them.

The real difficulty lies not in the meaning of these teachings, but in how we can do one without violating the other. How can we speak the truth but do so in a way that shows that we still love our neighbor? Or how can we wholeheartedly love our neighbor and at the same time speak the sometimes hard truths of the Gospel? Is that possible? Jesus thought so, and so did Paul. Therefore we must try.

We must not minimize, however, the difficulty of the task. We live in a new day, a postmodern day, where the old rules and old methods do not work. Most of the people in this new day are asking questions typified by the issues raised by David Payton, a University of Texas graduate student in electrical engineering, in a letter to the school newspaper, the *Daily Texan*: "There are millions of moral and ethical people who don't believe in Jesus Christ, but who nevertheless have made positive contributions by increasing the amount of joy or decreasing the amount of suffering in the world. Some of them follow the teachings of Judaism, Buddhism, Islam, and Hinduism, to name just a few. Others are atheists, agnostics, or humanists."[4] How does the Christian Gospel relate to these new, next-door neighbors? And how does what these good people believe and teach relate to us?

In each of the chapters that follow, I present a question that Christians are raising about how to deal with a religiously plural world. My task in each chapter is to show how the truth can be preached in love in the context of the question. The factor that makes this so difficult is the context. We have no single church authority, so we cannot just quote Augustine or Aquinas or Calvin or our pastor. We cannot simply cite canon law or the Book of Order. Since we are dealing with people who are searching for their own religious answers, we cannot simply give authority-tainted answers; we must marshal Scripture, theology, and prayer to find the specific application of "speaking the truth in love" (Eph. 4:15).

The following three chapters answer questions about how we should *think* about dealing with a religiously plural society, the next four give examples of what we should generally *do* about it, the next three tell how we should *witness*, and the final chapter sums up the challenge before us.

Part 1
Thinking Straight

THE CHRISTIAN ANSWER TO THE CHALLENGE OF pluralism starts with some straight thinking about the other religions. Since the other religions are with us, in our own neighborhoods, our relationship to them is not a theoretical question to be discussed in some Sunday school class on missions. It is a question of immediate, practical interest.

That practical interest, however, needs to be informed with a solid, clear-headed base. We start our search with some fundamental questions of how to approach the challenge of the world religions. Should we be afraid? If not, why not? What are the intentions of these religions? How aggressive are they going to be in attempting to further their own religious beliefs? Aren't the world religions trying to take over? If so, what should we do about it?

Maybe the intense competition signals a time for even more radical thinking. Maybe we should finally realize that religion is religion and the big deal we make over the different religions really is not that important anymore. If we could agree that religions are all the same, the conflict would disappear in a hurry. Or would it?

How we answer these basic questions makes a great difference when we start trying to answer more specific ones. We do not want to go wrong here, or our solutions to the other questions will be hopelessly confused.

2

Should I Fear the Challenge of These "New" Religions?

IT IS NEVER PLEASANT TO SEE A COMFORTABLE WAY of life slip away. I was in a seminar with several other scholars, and we were talking about the growing number of people from other religions in our neighborhoods. We had moved beyond the facts and were speculating on "what should be done."

Several suggestions were made, and then the oldest member of our group spoke up: "You know, if we do not do something, we'll see a way of life we have spent two hundred years developing here in the United States just disappear."

I have thought a lot about his comment. He is a very wise man, not an alarmist by any means. His comment reflected, I think, a fear common to most people who, for the first time, hear the facts of religious pluralism in our country. That fear is twofold.

First, we as Christians fear that we will lose our place of majority. The founders of our country were Christian, the governmental structures are all based on Christian principles, and the vast majority of people in this country have always been at least nominally Christian. Will religious pluralism change the comfortable advantages of that heritage?

Many fear that it will, and they are prepared to do something about it. Fear of non-Christian religions, indeed of religion in general, is a fact. Every year George Gallup does a poll in which he asks people to list the groups they would least like to have as neighbors. Five of the first eight groups mentioned in the 1988 survey were religious groups: religious sects and cults (44 percent), fundamentalists (13 percent), Jews (3 percent), Protestants (2 percent), and Catholics (1 percent).[1]

Although my scholar friend is not in the category of those who would discriminate against those of non-Christian religions, his basic fear is not an unusual one in the United States today. Many Christians have deep concerns about what is happening.

Second, the fear goes beyond simple numbers. The deeper fear is that all of the work we have done as Christians to "Christianize" our culture, to make it as much as possible a reflection of solid Christian principles, is liable to go up in smoke if people of other religions gain influence here. "I do not want my children to be learning values and morals that are at odds with those of the Christian faith," one pastor told me several years ago as he watched a Hindu temple being built two blocks from his home.

We should not belittle these fears. Many of the people who express them, like my scholar friend mentioned earlier, are solid, responsible Christians. They genuinely care about non-Christians and are not interested in causing them pain. They simply struggle with what to do in the face of growing religious pluralism.

Pluralism means, among other things, that the ideas our children hear and learn will be different from those we heard and learned as children. Philosophies more compatible with Eastern religious thought than with Christian theology have already found a home in our universities (where too often the task is to find ways to change Christian theology to match those philosophies rather than vice versa). Popular music, children's literature (including comic books), and movies (such as *Star Wars*) are as likely to reflect Hindu and Buddhist worldviews as Christian ones. Fear of pluralism does have a basis in fact.

The question is what to do about these facts. Should we respond in fear? Should we fight the trend? Should we reinstitute restrictive immigration laws? Should we consider protective legislation to insure that the United States remains a Christian nation?

I am not of the opinion that we should respond in fear. We should respond, of course, but not in fear. Let me tell you five reasons why fear is inappropriate.

1. The Christian Church Has Always Survived Pluralism

Consider the historical perspective. This is not the first time in history that the people of God, whether Israel or the New Testament church, have faced pluralistic situations. I once counted up the number of times the people of God in the Bible faced an alien worldview. I found more than 130 incidents, sometimes resulting in clashes of either a physical or intellectual nature, sometimes resulting in cooperation between the two groups.

A closer examination of these 130 "biblical pluralisms" revealed that God's people were often inconsistent in how they approached those of other religious traditions. Sometimes they disobeyed God's commands and fought them physically. Sometimes, especially in the Old Testament, they *obeyed* God's commands and fought them physically. Joshua, Saul, and David, for example, all took turns fighting the Canaanites in order to establish their control over the promised land. The fight was not purely religious; it was partly, perhaps mostly, political. But it was a fight, with hundreds on both sides dying.

On the other hand, David, and later his son Solomon, established a warm relationship with Hiram, a Phoenician king who traded with Israel and helped Solomon build the temple by supplying timber, the cedars of Lebanon. Note that Hiram was not a believer in Yahweh.

Thus, the people of God have related in very different

ways when confronted with people who believed differently. No standard rule book exists on how to act, although some interesting guidelines could probably be written.

The important point to note is that the people of Israel always survived. The work that God began with human beings, such as with Adam, Noah, Abraham, Moses, David, and Jesus, always prospered, at least when surveyed from the long view of history. The biblical story ends with the establishment of God's witness to the whole world, the church, and all the challenges of other worldviews and religious traditions did nothing to prevent this working of God in history from being accomplished.

The situation has not changed much in the two thousand years of church history since then. The incredible growth of the Christian community in that time period, resulting in one in three people in the world being Christian, is testimony enough that clashes with culture are not necessarily threats to the existence of the church.

2. Religious Challenges Sometimes Strengthen the Church

Christianity has never operated in a vacuum. Challenges to the Christian church have often come throughout history. Hostile cultures have always challenged the countercultural teachings of Jesus. Usually that challenge has included a spiritual alternative of its own.

One of the most pronounced of these spiritual challenges was the insistent territorial and religious expansion of the Muslim empires in the Middle East, Africa, Asia, and even parts of Europe from A.D. 700 to 1800. In the Middle East and Northern Africa, Islam replaced Christianity as the majority religion. The church, however, survived and thrives today in most of those countries. Christianity surfaced from this encounter as strong as ever.

In a more recent encounter, even the concerted political, military, economic, and ideological attempts of Marxism to stamp out the church—indeed, all religion—in the Soviet Union, China, and Eastern Europe have failed dramatically. In China the churches planted by Western missionaries in the first half of this century were feared lost when the communists took over. Recent studies have shown, however, that the church merely went underground and, despite the loss of missionaries and Western material support, even prospered. Conservative estimates put the number of Christians in China at millions, some say up to 50 million.

Or consider Vietnam. After the end of the Vietnam War in 1975, Western missionaries and church leaders left South Vietnam fearful that the 100,000 Protestant Christians they were leaving behind would disappear under the hard dictatorial, antireligious hand of Vietnamese Marxism. Yet in the ensuing period of time, the number of Christians in Vietnam has tripled to conservative estimates of 300,000. I recently spent time in one of these flourishing churches, packed to the rafters with gospel-singing Vietnamese.

The Christian church has emerged from these very pointed persecutions not only strong in its own right, but in many cases as the only viable institution available to reestablish the basic human rights of people in those regions. Marxism forced Russians to write moral checks against an ethical account that turned out to have insufficient funds. Today in Russia, even the former communist rulers are recruiting Western theologians, ethicists, and Christian sociologists to come teach in their universities, because they realize that Marxism has left their culture ethically bankrupt.

It would be folly to suggest that the Christian church in the United States will face any kind of physical threat from the world religions, but it is not folly to suggest that a competitive threat is real. To the extent that history can be used as a measure of what "threat" religious pluralism is in the world today, we would have to conclude that the Christian church can take care of itself. Or it is more accurate to say that God can take care of the church, as God's plan in this world dictates.

3. An Inevitable Element of Risk Resides in the Gospel

History does not guarantee that just because things have worked out well for the church in the past, the future holds more of the same. History teaches lessons, but the major lesson it teaches Christians is that God acts uniquely and freely in time. God acts, we react. Therefore, we do not know for sure what will happen. In a real sense our living of the Gospel entails risk. Two Bible stories help explain the parameters of this risky venture.

The first story comes in Jesus' teaching of a parable in Matthew 13. He tells the story of a farmer who plants wheat in his field and then discovers that weeds (planted by a jealous neighbor?) are growing amidst the grain. The farmer's field-hands come and ask him if he would like them to pull up the weeds. The farmer tells them not to, because by so doing they might endanger the real crop. Wait till the harvest, he tells them, and the separation will be done then.

The lesson? Neither the world nor the church will ever be freed from "weeds," from those who do not fully understand or embrace the Gospel story. In the context of our inquiry, those who hold non-Christian worldviews will be with us until Jesus comes again. The Christian viewpoint, according to this interpretation of the parable, will never be the only way of looking at things in this world.

This lesson is consistent, of course, with the Christian doctrine that all people are free to choose the answers they find most satisfying regarding life's ultimate questions. This doctrine, called free will, describes God's purposes in creating us. God wanted created beings who would be free to respond. He did not want to create robots, zombie-like creatures who would respond unthinkingly in reaction to commands.

To be sure, human beings have not always chosen well or wisely. In itself, this unwise choosing is a validating sign that God created us free to choose either right or wrong. A robot can never choose anything outside what it is programmed to do. Because we as human beings are not programmed, we sometimes choose poorly.

The non-Christian religions are products of this off-the-mark choosing. We all desire God because God made us in his image. In spite of this *imago dei,* we do not always choose to find God in the best way. Sometimes we miss the mark by just a little bit, other times by a lot. When we do not allow our choosing to be corrected by some outside force (God's gracious guidance), then wrong choices can be formalized in overall religious and cultural patterns that lead to well-motivated, partially true, but non-salvific religions. This is the theological lesson of the parable of the wheat and tares. Other religions will be with us always.

The second biblical example is the parable of the talents. In this parable the master gives each of his workers money to use as they wish while he goes away on a trip. One worker invests the talents and realizes a major increase, while another invests and gets a modest increase. A third worker, however, buries the money and returns it intact to the master when he comes home.

Upon his return, the master praises those who invested the money and took a chance. They could have lost the money by investing it. The story, however, pointedly asserts that that is what the master wanted. He did not want the money buried in the ground; he wanted it invested, even though this put the money at some risk.

The money in this parable parallels the Good News that our Master, God, has given us. We are not to bury this valuable gift in our churches; we are to invest it in the sometimes dangerous market of our secular culture, mixing it up with competing stories from the non-Christian worldviews wherever possible. That is the only venue, the open marketplace of the world, where we have a chance of realizing a strong return. If we keep it safe in our churches, this parable teaches us, we bury it with no hope of increasing its influence.

Both these parables teach us that the fundamental attitude toward the world and its non-Christian worldviews should be one of engagement. The mixture of Christian and non-Christian will always be with us, and the best way to approach that mixture is to try and change it for the better. Even though some risk may be involved, we can only transform the world if we are willing to engage. The parable of the talents indicates that such engagement will bring reward.

When we look at the growth of the non-Christian religions in our culture from this light, we should be anything but afraid. In fact, we should be pleased that we are in the midst of an environment where the Good News can be so effectively invested. Although we can still go overseas looking for "markets" in which to invest the Gospel, we also have a market of high potential return right here among us.

4. Who Said Loving Our Neighbors Would Be Safe—or Easy?

Nothing in the Bible promises that loving neighbors will be easy. In fact, the Bible teaches the opposite.

We are told that love is the highest law—higher than wisdom, higher than faith, the summary of all laws. Should we expect the highest law to be easy? The biblical examples we have of how to be loving seem difficult indeed: unquestioningly giving hospitality to travelers and aliens; loving neighbors as much as we love the most important person in the world (ourselves); loving outcasts such as the hated Samaritans; and even loving our enemies. It doesn't sound easy, does it?

So why should we think that loving those who belong to non-Christian religions should be easy? The command to love neighbors is unequivocal, but the Bible does not promise us a rose garden. We will be challenged every step of the way.

Loving such neighbors may be highly uncomfortable. Because these people believe differently about the most basic questions of life, we do not have a common starting place for our relationship with them. Christians and non-Christians are looking at different road maps of life, and the guidance we get from each often sends us in different directions. For example, suppose we invite a Hindu family to share a Fourth of July barbecue. It starts out to be a typical Fourth of July barbecue—hot dogs, hamburgers, chicken. But then we realize that our Hindu neighbors are vegetarian. Whoever heard of a Fourth of July barbecue with no meat? Shall we have barbecued asparagus or barbecued rice?

If this seems trite, the Bible tells a much more challenging story. The Good Samaritan interrupted his travel plans, broke a number of social taboos, and paid money he had no hope of recovering, all in the name of loving his neighbor. Loving neighbors can be uncomfortable.

Loving neighbors can also mean being rejected by those we try to love. In 1988 Terry Waite, an Anglican priest from England, put himself at great personal risk to try to negotiate peace with some Middle East Muslims. For his trouble he was kidnapped and held hostage until the close of 1991. So much for the great rewards of loving your neighbor, the Royal Law.

We may try to befriend Mormon neighbors, only to find that they do not want to be befriended. They may consider us apostate. They may not want their children to play with our children. Remember that they consider us non-Mormon even as we consider them non-Christian. Being rejected by the objects of our love can be painful.

Rejection, however, has an even more painful form. The reward we get for loving non-Christian neighbors may be rejection from other Christians who do not read the biblical command to love neighbors in the same way we do. Some Christians believe that the command to love neighbors applies only to the more acceptable variety—people who believe roughly the same things we believe. Those who do not believe as we do should be avoided.

Those who believe in avoiding non-Christians (indeed, even other Christians) can bring great pain to those who do not. A friend told me of a favorite uncle who belonged to such a group. When the uncle died, my friend's father was not allowed to preach at the funeral because he did not belong to the right Christian group. That kind of in-house rejection for loving one's neighbor can make the command a very difficult one to follow.

5. Our Majority Is Safe

In 1988 I took a trip to Egypt to find out how the church was faring on a steady diet of Muslim control. After talking to scores of Christians there, I heard countless stories of faithful Christian witness. The church was doing just fine. Conditions were difficult, but the church was strong.

My concern was further tempered by one particular conversation with Bishop Athanasius. After a few minutes of listening to our questions of concern (more than a little tinged with Western condescending superiority, I'm sure), this saintly man looked at us kindly and said, "Thank you for your concern. But please remember: the Christian church in Egypt has been here for almost two thousand years. The challenge of Islam is here, but we will survive. To be frank, we are more worried about how you will stand up to the challenge of Islam in the United States."

For me, this was an "Aha!" moment. We have been the dominant faith here for so long that we do not see the challenge, even when it is at our own doorstep. Instead of taking steps to meet that challenge, we are liable to overreact with fear, as if our faith, because we have tied it so closely to the fortunes of our nation, is in danger. We must see that the future of the church is in God's hands. Our task is to face daily the challenges that history, culture, and other religions place in our path. We must face them with dignity, confidence, and love—not with fear.

The feelings of comfort we get from being in the majority in a country like the United States should be considered a blessing, but sometimes it takes persecution to bring out the best of our faith. And often we fail to take advantage of the great blessings and opportunities that that majority gives us: resources to preach the Gospel well, freedom to believe what we want, and access to media and people everywhere. In our context, at least, fear is probably more a sign of laziness and doubt than of a real threat.

We should not be afraid of the non-Christian religions; we should be challenged by them. The only thing new about the challenge of non-Christian religions and worldviews is how we step up to that challenge, given the unique cultural situation of late twentieth-century America.

3

But Aren't the World Religions Trying to Take Over?

IF YOU HAD DRIVEN DOWN HIGHWAY I-35 BETWEEN San Antonio and Austin, Texas, in the spring of 1991, you could not help but see a large billboard at the side of the road that proclaimed in huge letters, "Vasectomy Reversals," and then in smaller letters a phone number and location. When I saw the billboard, my first thought was, *What a strange thing to advertise.* When I thought about all the other medical procedures one could trumpet, this one seemed minor. Who would be interested in emphasizing this particular kind of surgery? My imagination ran wild as I sought a logical answer. A building contractor could use the side of his office building to announce, "Shingles Cured." Or a plumber could advertise, "Hip Joints Replaced." Who would make a big advertising push for vasectomy reversals? And why?

It was not until I later talked with the pastor of a small church in a town not far from the site of the billboard that I heard the full story. Two doctors, members of Christian churches in the area, had started a ministry called "Renewed Blessing" to reverse tubal ligations and vasectomies surgically. From a brochure they published, I learned three things:

1. The surgeons involved were eminently qualified and medically above reproach.

2. It was not a money-making scheme. On the contrary,

the surgeons were especially interested in making the procedure as inexpensive as possible so that poorer families could afford it. They had made arrangements with the administrator of the local hospital to secure reduced hospital rates for patients seeking this treatment. The physicians had significantly lowered their own fees. They even arranged housing in local homes for those who had to travel long distances for the surgery. All in all, they had reduced the cost of the tubal ligation reversal procedure from $5,000 to $3,000. For men, a vasectomy reversal cost $1,500.

3. The motivation for the program was Christian. The brochure described couples who wanted a "second opportunity to bear Godly seed." The cover quoted Psalm 127:3, 5: "Sons are a heritage from the LORD, children a reward from him. . . . Blessed is the man whose quiver is full of them." In a lecture to a local women's group, one of the doctors expanded on his motivation: "We live in a dangerous, immoral world. . . . Christian values are in decline. . . . The numbers of Christians are in decline. . . . People like us need to be having children and raising them in Christian homes." The prime motivation was to increase the birthrate of Christians.

Several prominent people in our country have championed the idea of Christians increasing their birthrate. One surgeon involved in these procedures noted that his commitment to the program came following a conversation with a well-known teacher of traditional family values, who favored the idea.

Sometimes the idea is advocated over against a threat. Patrick Buchanan, former press secretary to President Reagan, now a newspaper columnist, and a 1992 presidential candidate as well, wrote an impassioned column warning Christians of the growth of the world's Muslim population. "Clearly, Islam is in the ascent in Africa, Asia, and the Middle East," he wrote. "In the West, devout Muslims are having children while in our secular societies the philosophy of Planned Parenthood takes hold, and the condom is king."[1] Others have noted that Muslims are having children at three times the rate of Christians worldwide. In the past fifty years, Islam has grown 500 percent, while Christians have increased their numbers by only 50 percent. Much of the growth is due to a higher birthrate among Muslim cultures.

The fear in these positions is palpable. Buchanan closed his column with a comment endorsing poet T. S. Eliot's remark that the West would end not with a bang, but a wimper: "Perhaps the wimper will be that of a Muslim child in its cradle."

Obviously, the question that lurks behind all these machinations is this: Are the non-Christian religions trying to take over the world? As it turns out, that question is at the root of many fears of the growth of non-Christian religions. We are afraid of the world religions because of their hostile intentions. They are growing, some at a faster rate than Christianity is growing. Is there a conspiracy afoot here? Is it fair to ascribe hostile motives to those of other faiths? If so, what should we do about it—outpopulate them?

What Is the Nature of the "Threat"?

Many of the world's non-Christian religions are missionary religions. They have corollaries to the Christian Great Commission, the command to "go and make disciples of all the nations" (Matt. 28:19). The Buddha put it this way: "Go, monks, preach the noble doctrine. Let not two of you go in the same direction." The Muslim Quran says, "Invite all to the way of the Lord with wise and beautiful preaching." The Unification Church of Sun Myung Moon demands that its followers practice what he calls indemnity, long hours of hard work and witnessing to pay back God for humanity's sin. Mormon young people spend two years in specific mission for the church, seeking converts to the Church of Jesus Christ of Latter-Day Saints. Clearly, we as Christians do not have the corner on evangelizing activity in the field of religion.

Just as Christians have many different opinions on how the Great Commission can best be fulfilled, so followers of other religious traditions have varying opinions on how their command to "go and make disciples" can best be carried out. If we were to try to categorize these opinions, at one end of the spectrum would be the "judges." Judges believe other religions are abberations of the god-urge and ought to be eradicated. One should have no contact with them other than the rather formal contact that is required for the presentation of one's view of religious truth. Once nonmembers are presented the truth, they either accept it or reject it, and that is the end of the contact.

At the other end of the spectrum are the "acceptors." Acceptors believe that other religions are simply different ways of seeing the same truth after which all are seeking. Since the goal is the same, why not let them go for it in the way they feel most comfortable. And they, hopefully, will let others go for it in a style that suits them. According to this viewpoint, the Great Commission and its other-religion equivalents are simply meant to encourage and enable people of other religions to be the best Hindus, Buddhists, Jews, Christians, Muslims, or whatever that they can be.

Judges and acceptors are as far apart as they can be when it comes to their goal. Judges want others to change their religion; acceptors want others to be the best they can be in whatever religion they choose. The only point that judges and acceptors hold in common is that each group thinks that its approach to this question is the right one, and it will not tolerate any other approach.

We might also describe two intermediary positions. "Friendly competitors" believe that those of other religions are wrong in how they view truth. These people believe that they need to tell others their view of truth, but that there is no need to be unfriendly about it. They can live in peace with members of other religions, even fellowship with them to a certain degree, but the competitive aspect must always be there. If the judges are the umpires in a baseball game and the acceptors do not even think there should be a game, the friendly competitors are the two opposing teams, each respecting the other's talents, well aware of each other's weaknesses, and committed to winning the game.

Self-styled "realists" hold a fourth position. Realists are the not-so-friendly competitors, like two baseball teams who hold grudges against each other. They have had a couple of bean-ball brawls in the past, and whenever they come near one another, warfare could break out at any moment. There is little respect between them. Realists believe that those on the other side are mostly blowing smoke when they say they have the answers to life's most difficult questions. In some cases they have borrowed ideas from the other side; in other cases they have made up ideas for human reasons, certainly not because of any authentic divine revelation. Realists not only question the other group's view of truth, they also have serious doubts about the sincerity of their motivations. Realists differ from judges at one major point: Whereas judges are absolutely sure that they know the truth, realists are not sure that anyone can really know the truth. In fact, realists feel very comfortable with their doubt about other religions largely because they are so realistic about the hypocrisy and weakness in their own. But even that does not dampen their enthusiasm. In a game where no one can really know the truth, why not do all one can to champion one's own cause?

The important thing to realize about our simplified schema is that every religion has its own judges, acceptors, friendly competitors, and realists. No one religion has a corner on judges, although sometimes fundamentalist Christians and Muslims seem to covet the honor. Nor does any one religion have a corner on acceptors, although Hindus and academic Christians seem sure that all Hindus and Christians should be. At any one time in a particular country, the religious leaders may make it appear that the "true religion" advocates one position or the other (I think, for example, of recent events in Iran). But when we look at the overall patterns and the theological teachings of each of the religions we have been considering, almost all of them include all four attitudes toward "evangelizing."

Islam, for example, is often viewed as the most aggressive evangelizing religion in the world. The Islamic concept of *jihad*, or holy war, is often interpreted as advocating conversion by the sword. Perhaps at some points in history it has been used that way. Today, however, there is a great deal of diversity among Muslim theologians on how the concept of *jihad* should be interpreted. Some, like Syed Muhammad Naquib Al-Attas, professor at the National University of Malaysia in Kuala Lumpur, take the judge's view of Christianity. He believes that Christianity is a religion hopelessly corrupted by the secularism of the day. Islam, he thinks, holds the key to humankind's religious future. Other Muslims do not agree, however. Fazlur Rahman, longtime professor of Islamic studies at the University of Chicago, could probably be best characterized as a friendly competitor, even an acceptor. He believed that the religions of the world can live together in peace.

Hinduism is sometimes seen as a religion uninterested in evangelization. Recent events both in India and in the United States would belie that description. In India several Hindu groups have adopted the judge's stance toward Christianity, Islam, and Sikhism. Hinduism, they believe, is the true religion (at least for Indians) and should be the religion of the land. A Hindu who wrote in this vein, Dayananda Sarasvati, claimed superiority for Vedic Hinduism, not only in the religious sphere, but also in the rational and scientific spheres. Mahatma Gandhi, on the other hand, was an acceptor. As the liberator of India, Gandhi never hid the fact that he was a high-caste Hindu. Yet he felt there was a place for all the religions in the world.

There are Muslims, Hindus, and, of course, Christians who hold all four positions in relation to other religions. The ones we hear about the most, because they are the vast majority, are the judges, friendly competitors, and realists, or those who believe that some form of evangelizing of those of other religions is required. We hear about them not only in foreign lands, but increasingly in the United States.

Other religions in the United States are doing the same things with our population that we have done in other countries by sending out missionaries to them. A significant percentage of the readers of this book have been visited in their own homes by Jehovah's Witnesses or have been handed tracts at airports by Hare Krishna representatives. Mormons claim that Mormonism is the fastest growing religion in the world. With mission programs required for all of their young people, they have a natural work force that is increasing the ranks of Mormons faster than any other religious group in America.

Hindus, Muslims, and Buddhists all have mission programs in the United States to spread the truth of the Vedas, Quran, and the Dhamma. One of the largest success stories in the world is the story of the Japanese Buddhist-based Soka Gakkai, a lay-led movement associated with Nicherin Shoshu Buddhism. Sometimes called the "Value Creation Society," Soka Gakkai uses an aggressive evangelism technique called *shakubuku*, which has led to the conversion of more than five million families in Japan and more than one million elsewhere in the world, a large percentage of which are in the United States.

In this sense, the religions are trying to "take over"—sometimes with a great deal of taste and sensitivity, but at other times with arrogance and pride. The attitudes of non-Christian missionaries are reminiscent of Christian missionary attitudes in their diversity. But religion—all religion—by its very nature is interested in spreading its influence.

We have already said that our response to the growing influence of non-Christian religions should not be one of fear, but that still leaves the field remarkably wide open for other possible responses. How should we respond to these evangelizing efforts that are so varied in style and attitude?

The Search for a Christian Response

One way to look at this question is to consider how religions grow. Even though numerical growth is a difficult concept for some Christians and must be approached carefully, let us concede for a moment that numerical growth is important and that we should be concerned about it. We have already recognized that some non-Christian religions are growing faster than Christianity is, even to the point where Christian growth is threatened. What should we do about it?

At least four reasons why a religion grows in a particular country come to mind: birthrate, immigration, government endorsement of that particular religion, and conversion. If our concern is to maintain or develop a Christian majority in any country, then these are four areas to consider. We can develop growth plans emphasizing one or all of them.

Birthrate

Growth plan number one would be to have more children born to Christian parents. We could return to the days of large families, accept the large cost of raising such families, downplay those who say the world is in danger of overpopulation, and trust the statistics that show that most children born to Christian parents remain in the Christian church. In this way we can attempt to outpopulate the other religions.

Clearly this is the option chosen by the Christian doctors discussed at the beginning of this chapter. In a personal interview, one of the doctors said that Satan has a plan to dilute Christian influence in the world. The feminist movement is part of that plan, leading to less interest among women in bearing children and to the general deterioration of the American home. He maintained that Planned Parenthood is another agency Satan is using in their claim that there is an overpopulation problem in the world. This is a "humanistic myth," he said, adding that all the people in the world could be put within the city limits of Jacksonville, Florida, without their even touching one another. Satan is trying to wipe out Christian values, and the "killing of Godly seed" is part of Satan's plan.

There are probably different ways of making the argument

in favor of larger Christian families, but no matter what form the argument takes, several problems arise. The most important is that it is difficult to see a clear biblical warrant for increasing the Christian population through any sort of numbers-conscious birthrate emphasis. The Bible does say to "be fruitful and multiply," but it also gives human beings the responsibility to care for the creation, to raise the children we do bring into the world in a humane manner, which in our day costs more and more to do. Overall, the Bible puts far more emphasis on the quality of faithfulness of existing Christians than mass-producing new ones. Children are a blessing, but they are also a responsibility that require the careful marshaling of the limited physical and psychological resources each of us has. Briefly, the Bible seems to say this about family size: having children is a good thing; raising children well is a prime responsibility; one should not have more children than one can raise well, if God has called you and your spouse to have children; and having children just to out-do the Muslims or any other group is not a good motivation, even if "they" are doing it.

Immigration

The second growth plan is through immigration. If there are not enough people of our religion in a particular country, let us move some more in from other countries that have plenty. That is one sure way to raise the numbers.

In the United States some Christians have become concerned over the rising numbers of Muslims from the Middle East and of Buddhists and Hindus from Asia, South Asia, and India who are coming to our shores. The numbers have increased dramatically in the past thirty years, partly because of relaxed immigration laws since the Immigration Act of 1965, which greatly reduced immigration quotas. Many of the quotas were reduced to allow greater numbers of Southeast Asians from Vietnam, Laos, and Cambodia to come here after our military ventures in that part of the world.

Several newspaper and magazine columnists have publicly raised the question of whether or not we should shut the door, or have it open only a tiny crack, to further immigration. The pluralism of ethnic and religious mix has gotten out of hand, they say, and it is time to stop the flow before the very nature of the United States is changed beyond repair.

At issue here, as many have pointed out, are two conflicting metaphors about what the "very nature of the United States" is. One image is that of the "melting pot," where immigrants come from all over the world and become not New Britishers, New Germans, New Scots, but Americans. Something happens here that motivates people to work for the common good of all, even if it means giving up their own rights and some of their cherished beliefs.

The second metaphor is that of "roots," and it emphasizes the individual human rights of all who come here, whether they are Asian, European, Middle Eastern, Central American, or African. All are equally protected under law, all have the right to maintain their cultural practices, and, in the case of religion, to worship as they please.

Both metaphors teach a great truth about American culture, and both should be embraced. But both can be overemphasized to the detriment of the weaker segments of society. The common good is often an excuse for maintaining the status quo and for not allowing minorities their full rights; the human rights argument is too often made without any regard for the common good.

Christianity emphasizes both metaphors. American Christians should argue that neither be given precedence. Biblical Christianity respects the rights of both individuals and groups. Just as individuals have free will to choose or reject God, so groups should be protected in their choice of religion.

This argument for free will means that for Christians immigration policy should be decided on questions other than religious ones. As long as both the common good and individual human rights are protected, immigration should be decided on political and economic grounds, not on religious grounds.

Government endorsement

Growth plan three is to make one particular religion the law of the land, or in its more modern form, to favor one religion over all the others. In political terms, this favoritism is called "establishing" religion. Religious favoritism is not allowed in the United States. The United States was founded by people looking for religious freedom. They were trying to escape the established churches of Europe—the French Catholics, the German Lutherans, and the British Anglicans. This desire for religious freedom is so clear in our founding documents and the results have been so gratifying (religious persecution is at a minimum in the United States) that it would seem that the issue is closed to further discussion.

However, that is not the case. Some say that the founders of our country were basically concerned about freedom of religion in terms of Christian denominations, not in terms of a pluralism of different religions. Today we have a new reality. It is not Congregationalism, Episcopalianism, Lutheranism, and Methodism we are confronting; it is all of the world's different religions. This is a new situation, they say, and we need to think seriously about establishing Christianity as the religion of the land—this time through law, not trusting the demographic realities to carry us through.

One group interested in Christian establishment, sometimes called the Reconstructionists, thinks that eventually we should do away with the laws under which our country now operates and reestablish Old Testament law as the law of the land. If it was good enough for Moses, it is good enough for us, they seem to be saying. Religious pluralism has gotten out of hand, and if we are not careful, the Christian values and principles upon which democracy rests will be lost. If that happens, democracy will no longer work. We will be up Pluralism Creek without a Christian paddle to guide our course, and we will be in the same boat the Third World is in: hopelessly diverse without any chance of consensus, an anarchy that will lead to poverty and endless conflict.

Not all groups go so far, of course. Some support much milder forms of Christian advocacy on the part of government. The doctors in our small Texas town probably fall into this group. The advantageous pricing structure they have set up at their hospital for reversing tubal ligations and vasectomies is a good case in point of small-scale religious favoritism. Even this level of favoritism is problematic. Why should this offering of beneficial public hospital rates be offered to patrons who choose this form of elective surgery? Does not this kind of favoritism subvert the basis of democracy—equal opportunity for all—just as surely as the loss of a base of Christian values? When the hospital administrator in this case was asked if he would offer special rates on tubal ligations and vasectomies to Christians who were concerned about the stewardship of the environment and chose to address the problem by limiting their family size, the administrator said no. He was convinced that increasing family size was a valid way of preparing godly persons to "take over."

Conversion

Growth plan four is conversion. We have in the United States the freest market of religious ideas anywhere in the world. The Constitution protects all expressions of religion. We all are free to do our thing. Let's just do it.

This argument is based on the idea that if our religion is the true one, and if we are really playing on a level playing field where all ideas are given free expression, then we should let the chips fall where they may. Let us do our evangelizing, let other religions do their evangelizing, and then watch what happens.

I think this fourth option is the one to choose. In some sense, non-Christian religions are trying to take over the world, if by that we mean that they are trying to convince other people to adopt their religion. But that is also what we as Christians are trying to do. That, after all, is the whole point of Christianity. So let's do it.

There are, however, fair and humane ways to do this mutual evangelizing. In Part 3 we will talk about what those ways are. But before we get to that, we need to discuss one additional problem: Remember the acceptors? They are the people who do not think any evangelizing from any of the religions is really necessary. Christians, Muslims, Jews, Hindus, Buddhists, Mormons, New Agers—all of them should simply do their thing with mutual encouragement from all and for all.

The number of acceptors in any of the religions is small, but their position is important and is growing in influence. Put in question form, what they are really asking is whether or not all religions are the same. If they are, what is the big deal about evangelizing each other anyway? One way to solve the clash of religions is to argue that the clash itself is based on misguided assumptions.

Is it?

4

Aren't All Religions Basically the Same Anyway?

MANY PEOPLE, SEEING OTHERS OF DIFFERENT religions moving into their neighborhoods, are asking the question in the true spirit of neighborliness, "Aren't all religions basically the same anyway?"

The development of this position is quite understandable and is often held by the very people whom we like and admire the most. It is frequently advocated by those who are extremely people-oriented, who take the command to love their neighbors seriously, who not only say they believe this command, but actually put their love into action. This admirable motive quickly leads these lovers to question the importance of religious differences. What is the big deal, anyway? Worship is worship, whether the object of worship is God, Allah, or Brahman. Prayer is prayer, no matter what name we give to the listening force. And so we are faced with a fundamental question about the world's religions: Are they all the same or not?

All Religions Do Address the Same Basic Human Need

When we examine various religions from the point of view of human needs, all of them are the same. We are created in such a way that we naturally search for a God in order to complete our existence, give meaning to the many experiences we have, and unify the diverse facets of human life. Human beings are incurably religious.

Perhaps this seems like a cut and dried assumption. *Sure all people are basically religious,* I can hear you say. *Just look at history. No society in the history of the world has ever, for any significant length of time, denied the essential importance of religion.* That observation is correct. All of history has an unvarying religious component. All people have been religious in one way or another.

Yet you will be surprised to know that at times in history the Christian church has challenged this seemingly obvious principle. One example is the missionary efforts of the church when the Spanish settled Mexico and Central America. Some European Christians questioned whether the people living in the New World were really created in God's image in the same way that Europeans were and whether they had the same religious needs. The church found it necessary to call a meeting, called the Council of the Fourteen, where theologians debated both sides of the issue.

Fortunately the theologians decided to side with the apostle Paul on the issue: "[Gentiles] show that the requirements of the law are written on their hearts, their consciences also bearing witness [to the law]" (Rom. 2:15). We have within us a natural sense of right and wrong, and it is that sense that convinces us that something is wrong with this life and that we need to seek help from an outside power. Thus, the God-search, the universal, unvarying human search for spiritual help, is born. In *this* sense, the root of all religions is the same, making all religions the same.

All Religions Are Equally Sincere

Instead of saying that all religions are equally sincere, we could equally say that all religions are equally insincere. Several modern Christian theologians have said that because religions are human-initiated attempts to find God, they are doomed to failure. Some include institutional Christianity in this assessment.

But I prefer the high road. The world's religions have done a great deal of good for humankind. Hinduism has given millions of Indians a reason for living, despite their over-populated, poverty-plagued conditions. The Buddha taught a balanced way of living between ostentatious materialism and self-hating asceticism. Christian missionaries have almost single-handedly raised the world's health quotient. Muslim philosophers preserved much of ancient Greek philosophy. Chinese religious culture, despite extraordinary diversity, has held together through that country's long and rich history. Despite being frequently used as tools of war, the world's religious institutions have consistently kept a concern for peace and love in front of our world's political leaders.

We often see attempts to prove the truth of religions based on which one has done more good in terms of humanitarian and political deeds. This is not the most effective way of proving the truth of a particular religion. It may be easy for Christians to point the finger at the Muslim invasions and conquests by the sword, at sexually promiscuous tantric Hinduism, and at the Japanese use of Shinto as a racially oriented nationalism. But Christians have their own history in these areas: witness the medieval Crusades, the Spanish Inquisition, and modern televangelist excesses.

The safer (and probably more historically accurate) approach is to admit that none of the world's religious institutions has been totally pure ethically. All have done a great deal of good, but all have stumbled badly at times. On balance, the religions that have survived have done so because they are motivated by good people seeking God or the gods in the best way they know how.

From this point of view too, all religions are pretty much the same.

All Religions Teach the Same Moral Code

If you look at the underlying "ten commandments" of each of the major world religions, you find a remarkable similarity. C. S. Lewis called this moral code the *tao*,[1] a universal code of morality that undergirds all the religious teachings of the world that have managed to last any length of time. In this sense, too, all religions are the same.

For example, both Buddhist laypeople and monks live by the *pancasila*, five rules of morality that form the foundation upon which the religious life is built. The *pancasila* disallows killing, stealing, lying, unfaithfulness in sexual relationships, and the taking of intoxicating substances. It is quickly evident that these five rules would be common to any religious code of behavior. Jeffrey Moses has shown in his book *Oneness* that these kinds of fundamental rules run across all religions.[2]

Most religious codes of behavior have minor differences, of course. Some are more elaborate than others. Monks in Buddhism, for example, actually live by a moral code that includes 227 rules of behavior, including the five of the *pancasila*. Confucius taught a rule of behavior that corresponds in principle to the Christian Golden Rule, "Do unto others as you would have them do unto you." But because in Confucianism the rule is changed slightly—"What you do not want done to yourself, do not do to others"—it is called the Silver Rule. These minor differences give religions their distinctive personality.

Sometimes the differences can be attributed more to cultural rather than to religious factors. Religious traditions have three different levels: the universal, the cultural, and the individual. Culture is the carrier of the universal ideas that make up the core of any religion and is also the structure that allows individuals to express their religious experiences. Culture is not identical to religion; it is a means of expression rather than the essence of the belief. Thus, differences should be expected. Christians in Eastern Orthodox churches, for example, use such "strange" practices as incense and icons in their worship, whereas Christians in some Western churches would never use either, preferring to rely on certain types of music and personal testimony to achieve the same worship goals. This is not because the Christianity of the two cultures is different; it is because Christianity takes a different cultural form.

In addition to different cultural forms, there can also be variety in the execution of a religion's moral code from culture to culture. In *The Day America Told The Truth*, James Patterson and Peter Kimit tell how their research for the book revealed that Americans do not follow the Ten Commandments of Christianity very closely. Ninety-one percent of Americans lie regularly at work and at home. Seven percent of those polled said that, if offered ten million dollars, they would kill a stranger. Nearly a third of all married Americans have had an affair.[3] Such things occur even though Christianity (with its Ten Commandments) is the religion of the majority of the American people. Surveys of other countries dominated by other religions would probably show the same laxity in the practice of religious morality.

Nevertheless, the moral core remains constant—and it is important. The common moral core is what many think can bring the religions together on projects of common concern: overcoming poverty, hunger, homelessness, secularism, war, crime, and other human problems. If we can agree on a fundamental moral code, we can more easily live with the deepest differences between religions. And there are deep differences.

Religions Differ in Their View of the Transcendent

A case can be made that all religions refer to a ruling force, a God, gods, or some transcendent principle. It is appropriate to define religion as that which invariably includes a transcendent principle so that adherents of that religion stand apart in some way from existence on a purely human level.

Some take this idea of all religions having some kind of transcendent and go a step further. Different cultures put different names and faces to this ultimate goal, they say, but in the end it is all the same goal. If this is true, then why should we quibble over the forms of our religions and their importance?

Two metaphors are often used to describe this argument. The first is the metaphor of the blind men and the elephant. Several blind men were once asked to describe an elephant. Since they were blind, they had to describe it by touch. One blind man grabbed the elephant by the trunk: "An elephant is like a snake," he concluded. Another grabbed the elephant's leg: "An elephant is like a tree trunk," he said. A third grabbed the elephant's tusk: "An elephant is smooth, hard, and cold," was his remark. All three were describing the same animal, but they came up with very different descriptions. Similarly, religions all describe the same thing, but because we are finite beings trying to describe the infinite (blind, so to speak), we each describe different aspects of the same truth.

A second metaphor uses the analogy of a journey. We all are climbing a mountain. The summit of the mountain is the same for us all, but each of us is taking a different path to the top.

Looked at from one way, there is some truth to this argument. The *function* of the transcendent in each religion is quite similar. It is the highest principle, and by either its action or its being that principle sets some kind of goal for the religion. But at that point the similarities end. If we examine each religion's transcendent principle closely, we find irreconcilable differences. The differences go far beyond names: Brahman, True Name, Isagami and Izagami, Yahweh, God, Allah, Enkai, Olodumare, Inkosi, Quetzalcoatl, Wakan Tanka.

First, transcendents differ in their very nature. The Brahman of Hinduism is not a person, but a principle or force that unifies all of creation. It is the underlying "Force" of the universe, to use the terms of the *Star Wars* movies. Contrast that with the very personal transcendent of the Muslim

Quran, Allah. Allah is an active agent, totally separate from human beings; there is no identification between created and creator in Islam as there tends to be in most forms of Hinduism. Brahman and Allah are impossible to reconcile unless you change the very nature of the two religions.

Second, the various transcendent principles of the different religions differ in what they do. Some of the transcendent principles simply exist. The Tao of Chinese thought is a principle of existence that explains the harmony of the created world in its ideal form. Contrast that with the very active God of Christianity who reaches down and grabs recalcitrant sinners by the scruff of the neck and offers them salvation through a gift of grace. And contrast him with the high gods of some African traditional religions who created the world and then "semi-retired" to let lesser spirits do the work of running the world. The gods of the world religions do different things.

Third, people respond to the transcendent principles in different ways. Adherents of the early Indian Vedic gods believed that they had to perform elaborate rituals and sacrifices in order to appease the gods and to tap into their power. Jews believe that God demands, above all else, obedience to the laws of the Torah. The Hindu Brahman and the Chinese Tao simply are, and adherents believe they must simply recognize the transcendent principle's nature and then get in tune with it.

Finally, not all religions will claim a transcendent principle. Theravada Buddhists do not believe in any god or theistic principle. They believe that it is up to each of us to find liberation by using the teaching of the Buddha to help us structure our quest. Modern quasi-religions such as Marxism and humanism have a similar response to the transcendent beings.

This extraordinary diversity makes it all but impossible to claim that all religions are the same.

Religions Offer Different Solutions to Human Problems

It is perhaps easiest to categorize religions as to whether they are self-help, God-help, or no-help religions. Self-help religions stress the action of the individual or community in setting things straight or achieving salvation, liberation, or freedom from the evils of existence. Perhaps the purest of all the self-help religions is Jainism. Mahavira, founder of Jainism and a contemporary of the Buddha, took the Hindu and Buddhist principle of *ahimsa*, or no-killing, and made it the cornerstone of his system for attaining Nirvana. Doing no harm to any living thing, animal or vegetable, became a way of gaining the necessary merit to clear karma-sullied souls so that they could be released from worldly existence. No one can help Jains with this task; they must do it for themselves.

Contrast Jainism with Reformation Protestant Christianity and Martin Luther's teaching that salvation comes by grace through faith and not through good works of any kind. This is the ultimate in God-help religion. Some forms of Mahayana Buddhism, especially the *bhakti*, or devotion traditions, have similarly stressed the gracious actions of a loving God to help us along our rock-strewn religious paths.

Some religious traditions hold little help at all. In a sense, "Be still and know that I am God" is the motto their adherents live by. Some Native American religions stress the oneness of human beings with the rest of creation and talk very little about an afterlife. The emphasis is on the harmony of all creation and the satisfactory living of life here and now, with little discussion of future rewards. No-help religions are not necessarily pessimistic, they are simply present-oriented.

The important point to note is that religions differ dramatically in their approach to the religious path. The religions prescribe different paths, lived for different purposes, with different destinies waiting at the end. There is little uniformity here.

So What?

In summary, there are some ways that all the religions of the world are the same: in their basic human motivation, in their sincerity, and in the common moral code that undergirds them all. However, the differences between religions are so drastic that it is hard to see how we could answer the question of this chapter in the affirmative.

The consequences of this are far more dramatic than simply responding negatively to the statement that all religions are the same. It means that any of us who take the religious questions of life seriously—Who am I? What am I doing here? Where am I going?—are forced to choose between the religious options offered by the world's religions.

But why do we have to choose? I can hear you saying. *Can't we just let people believe what they want? You believe what you want to believe, and I'll believe what I want to believe.*

From a purely human point of view that would be nice. It would be great if we did not have to disagree with our neighbors about anything, let alone something as important as religion. But it just does not work that way. Our minds are not constructed to allow for many different ultimate truths that do not agree with one another. They do allow for differences of opinions, of course, and we are allowed to be wrong or to have incomplete ideas of the truth.

But when it comes to truth itself, to what is *really* out there, regardless of our perceptions, opinions, or beliefs about it, there is only room for one truth. This is due to what philosophers have identified as the principle of noncontradiction. We cannot hold two statements as being true if they contradict one another. If we try to do that, then nothing can be convincingly determined to be true, including the statement that acceptors want to make about everyone having their own truth.

For example, if I point to a four-inch sphere and say, "That is an apple," and you and I understand what an apple is (a round, firm, edible fruit), and you point to the same object and say, "That is a baseball," and you and I understand what a baseball is (a round, firm, inedible toy), then both our statements cannot be true. The principle of noncontradiction says that we must choose one or the other (or neither—we both may be wrong). If we try to allow that both are true, then we really cannot identify any statement about the four-inch sphere to be true.

One option might be to say that the four-inch sphere can be whatever I want it to be, but that means that we are no longer talking about truth. We are now talking about my preference or feeling about an object. The object still is something or other. We have simply chosen not to try and determine what it really is. We want to make it whatever our imagination, at this moment, wants it to be. And tomorrow it may be something different.

Some individuals try to make religion fit this category of personal feeling. We must, however, be aware of the implications of this position. We are then saying the direct opposite of the question of this chapter. We are saying that all religions are different; we are saying that there are as many religions as there are people, and that none of them can be called true unless we define truth as individual and changeable.

We must also realize that none of the world's religions take this position. All religions claim truth for themselves. Each believes that the religious position it describes is true in the sense of corresponding to ultimate reality. This means that the religious system one describes can be communicated to others, and they can decide whether it is true or not. If they disagree, they must call it false. This decision for truth or falsity is what all the major religions of the world demand. All, by their very nature, claim truth.

Each of us is called to decide on the truth of religions. Religions are not all the same, yet each claims truth. And each of us must choose.

Part 2
Taking Action

SINCE WE ARE IN COMPETITION WITH RELIGIONS unlike Christianity, what does that mean to me? Should I read a book on the world's religions? Should I take a night class? Should I encourage my pastor to offer a Sunday school class on some of the implications?

Perhaps all of these will be options for you at one time or another, but none of them will be easily implemented. People have strong opinions on how the questions should be approached, and since the situation is new, we do not have a lot of church precedent to rely on.

This new challenge of the world religions touches on two of the most sensitive areas of life: our personal religious beliefs and how those beliefs can be expressed in the public arena. Everyone knows that, because they are explosive, religion and politics are not to be discussed in social settings where harmony is desired.

If you want an explosion, throw in the issue of the spiritual fate of our children. The world religions challenge not only our own faith and the spiritual climate of our community, but also the religious future of our children. No wonder we find it difficult to agree on these questions.

The following chapters look at some of the most difficult questions that pastors, parents, and children face in the churches and neighborhoods where you and I live out the most important parts of our lives.

5

If My Religion Is Right, Do I Really Need to Learn About Others?

EL CAMPO, A SMALL AGRICULTURAL COMMUNITY ON the Texas Gulf coast (population 5000), is not a cosmopolitan city. It is not a place where one would expect to find a great openness to studying the teachings of non-Christian religions. Sharyn Reynolds, a twenty-one-year-old graduate of the University of Texas in her first teaching job, did not realize that—but she soon found out.

Sharyn's discovery of this lack of openness began when several of her social studies students perceptively noted that the relationship between people's religious beliefs and the way they behave in political and cultural situations are much closer than the school textbooks seemed to recognize. They came to Sharyn and asked if she would be willing to organize an after-school discussion club to look at those questions. Thus the Philosophy Club was born.

Here is how it died. At their first meeting the nine students decided on subjects to study. They chose Hinduism, Buddhism, Islam, mystery religions, religion during the Civil War, and the causes of denominationalism, and then made assignments to one another. The next day Sharyn was called into the principal's office. A parent had complained, he told her, and when he heard the complaint, he agreed. In fact, he was shocked. What did Sharyn think she was doing, exposing these children to non-Christian values? She was to meet with the students and disband the club immediately.

"I was confused by a whole bunch of feelings," remembers Sharyn. "On the one hand, I felt shame—the principal had been my principal when I went to school there, and now he was angry with me. I respected authority and wanted to model my respect for authority to the kids.

"On the other hand, I knew that we were doing nothing wrong and that the educational goals of the class were 100 percent correct. We were going to study these religions for informational purposes only, to understand the world better. There was nothing wrong with that.

"Still, I knew that if I fought this too aggressively, I could be fired and probably would have great difficulty getting another job anywhere in the Texas Public School system. It was with these mixed feelings that I called the kids together and told them that we had to disband. They understood, and we never met again."

Should Christians Study Non-Christian Religions?

Sharyn had unwittingly run into a not uncommon feeling that non-Christian religions are dangerous to study. The fact that this was a small town in Texas in the 1960s makes little difference. The feeling can be found across America, and although recent Supreme Court decisions have encouraged more objective, informational study of the world's religions in the public schools, there are still deep antipathies toward it, particularly from parents of conservative Christian students. Like many strongly held antipathies, there are solid reasons for these feelings. Some are biblical, some are theological, and some are cultural. Some are good and some are not so good.

The cultural reasons hark back to the days when, separation of church and state notwithstanding, the social and cultural order was used to helping the church and family promote Christian values. Prayer opened public events such as Fourth of July picnics, high school graduations, inaugurations of public officials, and even school classes. No apologies were necessary for public school teachers to use biblical references as illustrations in classes and to be open and up front about their promoting the Christian religion in not so subtle ways. In fact, the community and parents counted on this as part of their children's Christian development.

Teaching about other, non-Christian religions in such a situation would be seen as a detriment to their children's Christian development. It would be like informing people on the features of Ford trucks when you are trying to sell Chevy trucks. The less said about the competition, the better.

The coming of real competition in the form of religious pluralism to our country as described in chapter 1 changed all that—at least officially. Religious freedom is for everyone, Christian and non-Christian alike, the law reads. This means that public and civic organizations cannot endorse any one religion even if it is the religion of the vast majority of the people—like Christianity is in El Campo, Texas.

However, the official demise of Christian civil religion, as this publicly endorsed Christianity was often called, did not put an end to the arguments against teaching other religions. Christians have other reasons, both biblical and theological, for not wanting instruction in non-Christian religions, and the question is whether or not religious pluralism has changed those reasons in any significant way. These reasons fall into four categories: the principalities and powers reason, the slippery slope to syncretism reason, the economy of resources reason, and the questionable commitment reason.

The Principalities and Powers Reason

Several biblical passages warn us against getting too close to the philosophies of the world. Colossians 2:8 is as good an example as any: "See to it that no one takes you captive through hollow and deceptive philosophy, which depends on human tradition and the basic principles of this world rather than on Christ." In other words, if it is not about Jesus, then it is worldly and we need to be careful of it.

This advice to avoid worldly philosophies is good advice, at least in a certain context. When we are talking about the principles we use to order our lives, the fact and meaning of Jesus Christ has to be the linchpin. The "principalities and powers" are forces that attempt to usurp the central place Jesus Christ has in our lives.

In the Colossians passage, the principalities and powers took a special form that probably included the following features, each of which challenged the type of salvation that the early Christian church offered through Jesus Christ: (1) Salvation was said to come through a special knowledge, sometimes secret, instead of through grace by faith in Jesus Christ. (2) There was a sharp dichotomy between the spiritual and material, which corresponded with a dichotomy between good and evil. The spiritual goal should be to escape the material in favor of the spiritual. Christ taught, however, that creation was good and at least partially redeemable from its fallen state. (3) Asceticism, not faithfulness, was the lifestyle of choice.

"Principalities and powers" can take many forms, but the key to judging their threat to us is whether or not they are accepted by us as usurping the core truths of Christianity.

That said, however, there are still many things in life we spend time studying that on the surface have little to do with Jesus Christ or with principalities and powers. Calculus, mathematics, fiction, and chemistry all can be studied quite profitably without mentioning Jesus and also without raising the principalities and powers question. Not everything we study has to be seen as a threat to the central truths of our lives. Not all subjects are of equal importance, nor do they have to be taught that way. So the question really is, can other religions be taught so that the principalities and powers question is not raised?

The answer to that question is complicated. It raises a theological question: To what extent do other religions represent human philosophies, and to what extent do they represent humankind's earnest seeking after God? Or some would even want to ask: To what extent does God use other religions to reveal portions of the truth? Many theologians point to a strong biblical tradition, based on Romans 1:20ff., that God has been revealed everywhere in creation. Even people who have never heard of God's name or of Jesus Christ's deeds sense God in the wonders and beauty of nature. This revelation is not enough to bring human beings to salvation, but it does mean that God can be found everywhere. I personally agree with this position, but there are some theological subtleties to it that allow many interpretations.

We do not have the space here to argue these theological subtleties, but let us distill a question that arises from the above question no matter what answer you give to it: If there are incorrect teachings in any aspect of non-Christian religions, whether partially or wholly wrong, is it better to try and avoid knowing about those teachings altogether, or is it better to study them, understand why they are incorrect, and compare them with the correct teachings?

It is probably obvious from the way I phrased the question that I think it is better to know about these teachings even though we disagree with much of them. I have two reasons for this.

First, it is almost impossible not to know about the teachings of other religions in some form or another today. Television, books, and popular music often have overt references to karma, Buddhism, Islam, Moonies, and others. Sometimes the references are accurate, sometimes not. But it is impossible in our pluralistic culture to avoid hearing these references. Even in El Campo, one hears. So, if the information is unavoidable, why not give it a controlled setting where at least we know that the information is accurate and as much as possible objective, with no hint of advocacy associated with it?

Second, the very nature of human knowing—of learning our own Christian doctrines, for example—is to compare and contrast them with examples of things they are not. I have three young sons, ages ten, twelve, and fourteen, and I have lately become conscious of how often they say something like, "Which do you like better, Dad, peanut butter or cinnamon on your toast?" When I tell them, the immediate follow-up question is "Why?" They ask similar questions about almost everything; it is obvious that they learn by comparing things. They rank, order, and value almost all of their experiences by comparing them.

My sons do the same with religion: "Which is better, Dad, Presbyterian or Baptist?" On a little different level, we adults also rely on comparison. For example, righteous behavior cannot be explained without having some concept of unrighteous behavior. Belief in God implies that there are those who do not believe in God. The idea of Jesus Christ being both God and man needs to be compared with both the idea of God and the idea of being human in order to begin to be understood. The list of uses for the comparisons we use in doing Christian theology are endless.

Why not use other religions as a way of teaching and learning Christian theology? Although that should not be its only purpose, it certainly is an inevitable side effect of studying other religions. Ask anyone who has spent sincere time studying another religion; they almost always will say that they learned as much about their own religion in the process as they did about the other religion. Readers will probably remember this argument as one used for studying a foreign language in high school.

If comparison is the essence of learning, we may as well use the concrete examples of other religions in our teaching. Pure theology tends toward abstractions that are difficult to understand; hypothetical contrasts ("strawmen," they are sometimes called) have an air of unreality about them that makes it difficult to take the point of the lesson seriously.

The Slippery Slope to Syncretism Reason

This question is often phrased this way: Does not the study of non-Christian religions increase the chance that students will incorporate elements of it in their Christianity?

We would be foolish not to recognize this as a possibility. It surely does happen sometimes. But studies of how syncretism, the adding of nontraditional religious material to a religious tradition, actually takes place would indicate that the adding of nontraditional material happens more frequently when the prevailing cultural influences are not understood or articulated.

Syncretism is a complex phenomenon that requires a number of factors to be present before it occurs. The clash of cultures, the perceived dissatisfaction with the existing religion, and a certain relativizing of truth (an abandonment of absolute truth standards) are required before syncretism takes place. Modern examples might be some of the new African independent churches which combine African traditional religion and Christianity. In the United States an example might be the Unification church, a combination of Korean shamanism, Mahayana Buddhism, and missionary Presbyterianism. Other examples could be cited, but their complexity makes analysis difficult here.

Because of this complexity, the slippery slope to syncretism danger seems pretty farfetched. Syncretism usually takes place in a slow, insidious process rather than as an act of conscious choosing. The unconscious process, fueled by massive social and economic as well as religious factors, that syncretism usually takes would argue for studying the world religions in a fair and objective manner rather than not. Unhealthy additions usually do not seem unhealthy when they are added. Often they are added because the full implications of their origin and meaning are not known.

Several years ago the Sunday school class of a prominent church with which I became acquainted decided to study meditation. A lawyer in the congregation was chosen as teacher. She was chosen because she had often talked about her good experiences with meditation: it helped her relax, she felt better physically, and she came closer to God. In her meditation she used Hindu, Buddhist, and Taoist techniques, as well as Roman Catholic and Protestant traditions of Christian meditation. In the teaching of the class she presented all of these traditions, used films to illustrate their practice, and shared her personal experiences with each.

Several in the class objected to her use of techniques of other religions for something as spiritually powerful as communion with God. Others saw little difference between the meditation being described and their practice of quiet time. All were interested in what she had to say, perhaps because she was an excellent teacher and was not defensive about her own practice, but perhaps also because they learned something of importance.

One of my students decided to study this class and its effects on the church. At the end, she summed up the results of the class with these observations:

- the class did not lead to wholesale adoptions of the meditation practices of the teacher;
- interest in the subject was intense; attendance was high;
- several in the class commented that they better understood what they were doing when they prayed to God because of what they learned in the class;
- it did not appear to upset the more conservative members of the church once they understood the goals of the class. The Christian teachings on communication with God were enhanced, and the potential for syncretistic adoption of incompatible theories of meditation, at least in this area, seemed even more remote than before the class.

The danger of syncretism seems to be much higher in a climate of ignorance than in a climate of full awareness. Several years ago, the movie *Star Wars* was popular with young people. The characters in the movie tried to tap into a mystical power source, called the Force, that controlled the universe. "May the Force be with you," became a catch phrase for young people. In fact, the idea of the Force is a dead ringer for the Eastern monistic, pantheistic view of God. Most of us would be savvy enough to reject pantheism, but some of us might be willing to use a cultural icon like the Force as an analogy for God unless we fully understood its implications.

Studying the world religions will in the long run lessen the chance of unwanted syncretism rather than increase it.

The Economy of Resources Reason

Immediately after Austin Presbyterian Theological Seminary decided to establish a teaching position in comparative religions and I was chosen to inaugurate the post, I was discussing the move with a Presbyterian pastor who had been a long time supporter of the seminary. "It seems like the students already have so much to learn about Christian doctrine," he said. "In fact, some of us think that not enough is being done in that area now. Now we're adding a whole new subject area when there is precious little room in the curriculum for the existing required courses."

His comments were good and sincere, born not of a reactionary spirit but of simple concern for the best way to prepare men and women for ministry. On one point he was correct: the modern seminary student has a lot to learn. Therefore I have had to give his comments a lot of thought. Is teaching world religions to seminary students a wise use of their time and of the seminary's resources? And by extension, does it serve the church well?

To answer this question, we must assess two things: first, the cultural conditions under which we live. Christian theology is never done in a cultural vacuum, and a principle fact of modern living is an increasingly free interchange of ideas between religions. This is a cultural condition that has never before been as true as it is today. To do Christian theology and not see it in that context would be to do a theology that might be applicable for the United States in 1890 but not in 1990. It would be a useless, or worse, false theology. Like it or not, the theology that the church needs now is a theology that takes pluralism into consideration. Such a theology demands an accurate, objective understanding of the world's religions.

Second, an old saying in religious studies says, "When you are studying other religions you are really studying your own." The "father" of the scholarly study of religion, Max Mueller, put it a bit differently: "He who knows [only] one religion knows none." Far from distracting us from learning about our own religion, the study of non-Christian religions actually enhances it.

There is another aspect to the economy of resources argument. That is the use of resources in their most concrete sense: dollars and cents. Is it wise to use our already short supply of money in efforts that do not directly support the cause of Christ in the world? This aspect of the argument actually blends into the next section, so we will address it there.

The Questionable Commitment Reason

Some think that Christians interested in studying other religions are somehow deficient in their own commitment to Christianity. This may take the form of a conscious desire to downplay the uniqueness of Christianity as a path to salvation, or it may be unconscious—a kind of Freudian death wish that we carry around, unknowingly sabotaging the acts of commitment common to committed Christians. As proof, people who hold this position cite the numerous instances of Christians, both scholarly and lay, who have become interested in the study of other religions and, apparently because of that study, have lost their orientation to the historic Christian faith. What surfaced, perhaps, were underlying doubts about Christianity that had subconsciously nagged at them all along.

There are enough of these cases that the criticism must be taken seriously.

Unfortunately, it is one of those criticisms that cannot really be negated finally. It is a your-guess-is-as-good-as-mine situation, mostly because it deals with human motivations, which are often tricky to discern. In the end the argument demands that one prove that the opposite is true—that the benefits of studying the other world religions far outweigh any alleged deficiencies—and try to show that the motivations that produce those benefits must be good ones. This is an equally difficult argument to prove, but at least it shows that the motivational case can be argued both ways: there are many instances of committed Christians who have undertaken the objective study of the world religions and have remained committed Christians and fine scholars of religion. That may not dispel doubts, but it does show that the argument can cut both ways.

It is more helpful to consider a specific form of the argument; for example, studying the other religions diminishes the commitment to Christian mission efforts. This argument ignores the positive benefits that a study of world religions can have for missionaries. It assumes that knowing a lot about other religions means that the Gospel can be less effectively presented. Almost all missionaries I know say just the opposite—that knowing what others believe helps in the presentation of the Good News because we are less offensive in how we present the Gospel; and the fact that we have spent time understanding their position demonstrates a sensitivity and concern that impresses non-Christians with the Gospel. It is true that not everyone who learns about the religious beliefs of others is interested in or believes in the evangelizing of non-Christians, but that is not a result of wanting to know more about other religions. In almost all cases it precedes it. Furthermore, wanting to know about other religions does not logically demand a lessening of the evangelistic drive—just the opposite may be true. Missionary annals are full of stories of missionaries who remained good evangelists and who also became experts in the religion of the people with whom they worked.

Second, the argument seems to imply that getting to know other religions suggests that we will be less aggressive in our evangelizing efforts. This is like the no-fraternizing rule that baseball teams have: Do not talk to the opposition before the ball game, because you will be less competitive once the game begins. Actually, I do not know a lot of missionaries or missiologists who would articulate this position, but just in case some would, let me say that this is a real perversion of what it means to be an evangelist. The essence of evangelism is love and care, not scalp hunting (or even game winning). We are witnesses to the truth, not the determiners of ultimate destinies. We can afford to be bold in our proclamations, yet gentle in our love.

Consider a second specific argument: Name the good that comes from learning about other religions. There are many answers here, but one that is crucial in our world situation today is the need for world peace. As of this writing, there are thirty-two shooting wars going on in the world today. Of those wars, at least sixteen are strongly identified as religious. Sikhs and Hindus in India, Muslims and Jews in the Middle East, Christians and adherents of traditional religions in Africa, Hindus and Buddhists in Sri Lanka, and Muslims and Christians in about six African countries. That the agencies in this world most committed to fostering love and community are so actively identified (usually used by politicians) with the worst thing that can happen in human societies is not a good thing. As one scholar recently put it, "There will be no peace among the nations of the world until there is peace among the religions of the world." Will not learning about and promoting the fair and objective understanding of other religions help us toward that goal?

Good things happen when we learn about other religions. We learn about other belief systems, enrich our understanding of our own beliefs, and learn that we have some common social goals with those of other faiths.

But learning about other religions does not stop there; the learning process almost always brings us into contact with people who believe the teachings of these religions. Can that possibly be a good thing? This topic is explored in the next chapter.

6

Doesn't the Bible Teach Us to Avoid Personal Contact with Non-Christians?

WHENEVER THE TOPIC OF PERSONAL CONTACT WITH unbelievers comes up, some point to passages such as 2 Corinthians 6:14–17 to argue against such contact. Fundamentalists use this passage to justify their doctrine of separation not only from unbelievers, but also from other Christians who do not belong to their fellowship. The Amish and some Mennonites use the passage, among others, to justify their physical separateness from modern life. And some—fundamentalists, Amish, and Mennonites included—use the passage to advocate no contact whatsoever with members of non-Christian religions. Obviously this is an important passage to consider in answering the question posed in this chapter.

The passage reads:

> Do not be yoked together with unbelievers. For what do righteousness and wickedness have in common? Or what fellowship can light have with darkness? What harmony is there between Christ and Belial? What does a believer have in common with an unbeliever? What agreement is there between the temple of God and idols? . . . "Therefore come out from them and be separate," says the Lord.

Like many key Scripture passages, 2 Corinthians 6:14–17 has been interpreted in a number of ways. One way is to understand this in the context of the first-century Corinthian church where Christianity was a new, struggling religion needing all the purity it could muster to survive. Since we do not have that situation today, such interpreters insist, the text does not really apply to us. A second way is to distill a foundational principle from the text that works in all cultures and at all times—*Don't associate with unbelievers*—and apply it as one would apply a law against speeding: *Don't* ever *do this.* A third way is to come to the text with a modern need—for example, a reason to emphasize the importance of religion as a factor in successful marriages—and find in it a passage that disallows mixed marriages.

What does this text mean for us? Nothing? Is it an argument for separation? A warning against mixed marriages?

I do not know if a minister whom I will call Arthur Brown (you will soon see why we disguise his name and some details of his story) has ever done a detailed exegesis on 2 Corinthians 6:14–17, but he has certainly thought through the issues involved. Arthur was a missionary to Guatemala for twenty years, and it was in Guatemala that he and his wife, Lois, raised seven children—three boys and four girls.

"I think the experience was a good one for the kids," remembers Arthur. "Our church experience at that time was quite pietistic, but the church gave the kids both Bible study and recreation. The kids were very much into the church we were helping to begin. We kept them at home for their education, using correspondence courses from the United States. The problems did not begin until we returned to the States."

Arthur took a church job in the United States, and problems arose with their second son, Tom. "In a way it was surprising that it was Tom," said Arthur. "He was the only one interested in the ministry. He taught Sunday school, and when he was in the tenth grade he wrote the church Easter play. But maybe his own needs were not being met. The church I pastored had a small youth group with very few kids his age. Maybe we should have looked for a church with more young people. A strong youth program might have made a difference."

The reason for the second guessing is that Tom went to a state university, began to study Eastern philosophies, and, along with some other students, began to experiment with non-Christian religious experiences.

Arthur continued, "The school was a couple of hundred miles from the town our church was in, so for the eight years it took Tom to finish college, we were trying to keep tabs on things long distance. He took eight years because he had to support himself; in the evenings, he kept the books for a small pet food company. First thing we knew, he had dropped out of the church we had served. He tried an Orthodox church for a while but eventually stopped going there also.

"On our visits I tried talking religion with him, but our views clashed so greatly that we finally stopped discussing religion. He was using philosophical arguments I did not know anything about. He married, he divorced, he married again. You know, when you raise seven kids, you begin to understand rebellion. They all go through some of it. But with Tom it has been twelve years of religious searching, and I just wish I could have helped him more."

When Arthur and I talked, Tom had just left for India to spend a few months studying with a guru on a communal farm. Arthur was reading books on Hinduism to try and catch up with his son's religious pilgrimage, and he and his wife were asking themselves a lot of questions about what they might have done differently.

"We often ask ourselves the youth group question I mentioned earlier. Sometimes I wonder if we should have had him go to a small Christian college before he went to the university. When Tom first started this quest, I said to him, 'You've been brainwashed by your professor.' But now I have mixed feelings about that. I do not know that I can blame one course for what happened. I know that Tom is still seeking, so I still have my hopes. I just hope he finds the truth."

What would Arthur Brown see in 2 Corinthians 6:14–17?

I did not ask him to do exegesis, but from what he said, I do not think he would have agreed with any of the three options we suggested above as possible ways of understanding the text.

Since he believes in finding modern application for biblical texts, he would think the text has something to teach us, especially since it appears to deal with a problem like his own. Like thousands of other American parents, he has felt the pain of a child rejecting the family's traditional religion in favor of another. So the question of relationships and influences of non-Christian religions is one to which he has given a great deal of thought.

When I met Arthur he was reading books on Hinduism ("I have enjoyed them; they don't turn me off."), so total separation is not the answer, at least as far as Arthur is concerned. When asked what he would advise other parents to do to avoid his experience, one of the things he mentioned is to study other religious traditions in the context of the church so that young people can be prepared for the pluralistic world they will be facing. "They need to learn discernment in the Christian context," is the way Arthur phrased it.

In fact, Arthur often mentioned the church as the context in which his situation could have been solved. And maybe that is as big a clue for how we should do our exegesis of this passage as any. What we need in order to understand a text like this (or any text) is a culture in which its teaching can be reheard. It needs to be a culture where the worldview assumptions will be the same as those of the New Testament church—or at least roughly parallel. Frankly, the church is the only possible place today where those worldview assumptions (the existence of a personal God who cares about us and wants us to behave in a way consistent with God's nature) have any chance of application.

This passage can be understood only in a culture where obedience, not self-interest, predominates. We need a culture where God is real, personal, and active, not abstract, disengaged, and distant. We need a culture dedicated to transforming the world according to the Christlike model, not a world that conforms itself to personal experience and greed. It is only in such a world that the message of the text can be lived. That world today must be found in the culture fostered by the church.

In such a culture, there may be times when separation from the philosophies of the world may have merit. However, there will also be times when the philosophies of the world demand contact, interaction, and even adoption. In such a culture we learn that separation is not the issue; the issue is the functioning of this community in a way that it can best fulfill its mandate.

What was Paul's message to the Corinthian church, and how can that message best be heard in the context of the modern church?

Paul's Message to the Corinthian Church

In order to understand 2 Corinthians 6, we must see how Paul led up to that chapter in his exhortation to the Corinthian Christians. Paul was writing to a church that had experienced some pain. We do not know exactly what the pain was, but part of it had to do with Paul himself and his expectations for the church. It apparently had to do with a teacher or teachers who led them astray. It surely had to do with spiritual growing pains. This was, after all, a young church with young Christians, and they were feeling their way. Growth often involves pain.

Paul wanted his letter to address the pain and to offer comfort. In the first few verses, he makes a point of recognizing God as someone who comforts us in all our afflictions. Paul had experienced this comfort himself when things had not gone well for him, and he wanted his friends in Corinth to know they too could find relief.

The relief comes not from a guarantee that suffering will never come again. No, indeed. Suffering is part of the game. Being a follower of Christ insures some suffering. Comfort comes first of all from recognizing that we are not especially singled out for pain; we are all subject to it.

Second, comfort comes from knowing that following God not only brings suffering, but it brings consolation as well: "Just as the sufferings of Christ flow over into our lives, so also through Christ our comfort overflows. If we are distressed, it is for your comfort and salvation" (2 Cor. 1:5–6), not just for some perverse reason or for the luck of life's draw.

By early establishing this dichotomy—suffering/ consolation—Paul sets up an important relationship that is necessary for understanding everything else he says. In the following verses of 2 Corinthians, he uses this dichotomy to explain many things about the Christian life. He uses his own experiences as an apostle (as *their* apostle) as the story to carry this teaching along, but for us the important part of this teaching is the message, not the story.

As sure as consolation follows suffering for the Christian, Paul says, so life follows death (2 Cor. 4:7–5:15). Before knowing Christ, we were consigned to death, but now that we know Christ, we are given life. Notice a movement here from the most general and abstract (suffering/consolation) to the human biological sphere (death/life).

Paul then gets even more specific. He brings it down to the level of the individual. Before knowing Christ you were an old person; now you are a new person (2 Cor. 5:17). Each of us, when we become a Christian, becomes a new person. We leave an old person behind and are transformed into a new person. This means that the way we look at our former deeds is changed. Before we were nice to our neighbors because they would then be nice to us; now we are nice to our neighbors because they, too, are children of God, and God commands us to be nice. Similarly, our whole lives are transformed into something new, something righteous.

Now we come to the core of the problem that some of the people at Corinth had, the problem Paul is really addressing and the key to understanding 2 Corinthians 6:14–17. Some people who had undergone this change from old person to new person were having withdrawal pains. Their old way of life may have led to death, but it had some good things about it. For instance, there were fun times. It was familiar, and because it was familiar, it was comfortable. Thus some of these "new creatures" were wondering if maybe there might not be a way of combining some of the good things of the old way of life with the indisputably better way of life that comes from knowing Christ. They claimed, as it were: "Understand that we are not talking about totally reneging on the new way. We are still convinced that that is best. If, however, we could just hang on to some of the old familiar things, the transition might not be quite so difficult."

That is really the point of 2 Corinthians 6:14–17. We must totally separate ourselves from the old way of looking at life. Our new, righteous way of living has nothing to do with that. There is simply no way to combine the two. They are radically different ways of looking at the world, and to try and do both would require having a Janus-like head, a face that looks in two different ways at once. There is no way of combining the outlook of each. We must choose.

The Way the Message Worked

Paul gets specific, and in his specificity we learn the lessons of this new way of looking at life.

Total Dedication. We must be totally dedicated to the ministry demanded by this new way of looking at life. Paul says that we must give offense to no one. In another place he talks about becoming all things to all people (1 Cor. 9:19–23). We must endure all things that might come our way because of this ministry. There is no ducking; we cannot say that this is our ministry and then not be prepared to endure the consequences. The consequences may be good or they may be bad, but make no mistake: being ambassadors for Christ has consequences. Remember, though, that for every suffering, there is a corresponding consolation.

Total Focus. Because of this new life, a clean break with

the past is required. To try to combine the two would lead to being "yoked together with unbelievers"—your old friends are now unbelievers, who now look at things totally different from the way you do. There is no combining those two outlooks, for they are incompatible. One is righteous, one is not, so do not try to combine the two.

Notice that this is not a rejection of unbelievers as people, nor is it a rejection of any contact with them. It is simply Paul's way of illustrating the implications of the choice that the Corinthians have made to go a new direction. We can still be friends with these people and have fellowship with them. Jesus, after all, ate with publicans and sinners. Just do not fail to remember that there is a substantive difference between you and unbelievers. You are now different.

This is not a call for separation in the legal or physical sense (as a strict rule). There may be times for such separation, but it is not a hard and fast commandment; it is a call for recognition of the metaphysical separation that our commitment to Christ entails. We have a new way of looking at the world, a way of the Spirit, not of the flesh, a way that leads to light and not to darkness, to life and not to death. Do not try to yoke this new way of life with the old way of life.

The Message to the Pluralist United States

How does this passage apply to Peoria? Does this kind of discussion help us with the situations we face in trying to decide as conscientious Christians what kind of and how much contact to have with non-Christians? Does it help Arthur Brown in trying to figure out what went wrong?

It does suggest some guidelines to consider when faced with a pluralistic situation. The approach that Paul teaches would seem to include answering five key questions.

1. Does this contact jeopardize my commitment to the new creation? If yes, temporary withdrawal may be necessary. For example, my immature faith may be unable to withstand such contact right now. In such a case, withdrawal has not so much to do with the situation as it does with my own faltering steps toward putting on the new person, the new life in Christ. Perhaps this will change, but right now I am unable to make this contact in a useful manner.

Or perhaps I am at a point in my life when I need to spend time alone with God. I need solitude with my Lord, just as Jesus often withdrew to pray. I need those times to recharge my spiritual batteries. Separation at such a time is a positive step toward spiritual growth, not a defensive step of fear.

2. Does this contact jeopardize my brother's or sister's commitment to the new creation? Sometimes babes in the faith need to be protected as they learn to digest the warm milk of new faith. They are not ready for the steak and potatoes diet of pluralistic contact. It is possible that interfaith contact will never be comfortable for some. Some might be called to it while others are not. The community should make the decision. Separation is not a rule for these people; it is simply a wise use of their calling and ministry talents.

3. Will Jesus Christ be glorified by this contact? The hostility of some contact may make it unwise. We should not feel compelled to make contact in physically or spiritually threatening circumstances. Yet God does not want us to be timid in contact. As we have seen, God expects the talents of the Word to be risked in the spiritual marketplace of the world in the hopes of high returns. On the other hand, God does not necessarily depend on us for getting his will done. God may have other plans, and the obvious danger inherent in a situation may be a warning against closer contact.

4. Will the church be glorified by this contact? As the church in the world we have a mission, and sometimes that mission coincides with the mission of other religions. Feeding the poor, helping the sick, and freeing the captives are teachings of all the great world religions. Sometimes we can join hands in accomplishing those things. When a church asks itself whether or not to get involved in such a ministry, the following should be considered.

What is the other group's attitude toward Jesus Christ? Basic respect for the teachings and work of Jesus Christ is a requirement. It seems unlikely that anything profitable will come from working with people who think Jesus was a fake or who have no respect for what he did. It would be a bad witness for us to do so.

Will the methods used and the results obtained in this collaboration be something we can be proud of? Measure them against the fruit of the Spirit in Galatians 6:22–23. We do not want to be involved in anything that will reflect negatively on the witness of the body of Christ.

5. Will the non-Christians I am involved with be helped by this contact? Some kinds of contact will not reflect positively on others. Overly aggressive or manipulative evangelistic campaigns hurt rather than help those who belong to non-Christian religious traditions. The "do no harm" principle of physicians regarding medical treatment is a useful one to consider in concert with the other four principles.

The apostle Paul's primary consideration was making sure that the people of the church at Corinth knew that being a Christian meant looking at life in a new way. Once that was established, fellowship with non-Christians took on a new meaning. In the context of that new meaning, there would be some situations where contact might be a good thing and some where contact might be a bad thing.

We should evaluate our own contacts in the same way. As long as we are looking at the world through transformed Christian eyes, contacts with those of other religions have great potential. We live in a culture and a world where making such contacts has never been more important.

The key to successful contact is belonging to a community of believers where the new way of looking at life, the transformed worldview, is assumed and supported. From such a base, the question of whether or not to have fellowship with non-Christian religions becomes much easier to answer in the affirmative.

7

Should I Let My Children Play with Children from Families Who Believe in a Non-Christian Religion?

MY SON DAVID IS FOURTEEN YEARS OLD. LAST YEAR each of his two closest friends, Jordan and Amitav, went through a religious ceremony that initiated them into the adult communities of their religious tradition. Neither was baptized. Neither went through a confirmation class. Those are Christian ceremonies, and neither Jordan nor Amitav is Christian.

Jordan, a Jewish boy, had his bar mitzvah. In Judaism, a boy reaches adulthood on his thirteenth birthday. At this time he is responsible for following the Torah, or the commandments of the law, just as all adult Jews follow it. A ceremony observes this time: the boy participates in a worship service, reading from the Torah and reciting blessings for the people. The service is followed by a festive party.

Amitav, who is Hindu, had his initiation into adulthood, called *upanayana*. It is sometimes called the sacred thread ceremony, because of the practice of giving the adolescent boy a thread consisting of three cords, which is worn over the left shoulder and hangs under the right arm. It represents to everyone that the wearer of the sacred thread is ready to assume the social and religious responsibilities of the adult world.

Both Jordan and Amitav invited David to attend their

ceremonies. David wanted to go, and he asked my wife, Judy, and me what we thought. We decided he could go.

I do not remember the decision being a particularly difficult one, yet as I think back to the factors that went into it, I have decided that it was both an important decision and one that had some subtlety to it. Choosing what kinds of non-Christian experiences we allow our children to be exposed to is not a cut-and-dried affair.

In one sense, this decision is a specialized case of the one we discussed in the last chapter. Our conclusion there was that the Bible teaches that separation from the world of the non-Christian should not be postulated as an ironclad rule. The freedom to engage the non-Christian world, however, is not an indiscriminate thing. Several factors need to be taken into consideration. In the case of children, those factors take on a special focus.

Protect and Prepare

The reason this is a particularly difficult form of the question is because of the nature of the parenting task. Not only is parenting difficult, but its emphasis changes almost daily. Let us examine those changing emphases this way: There are two main tasks involved in parenting. One is to protect our children; the other is to prepare them.

We protect our children from the vicissitudes of life:

- We do not want them to be overwhelmed with the needs of making a living, finding shelter, and keeping warm, so we provide them with food, a house to live in, and clothes.
- We do not want them to have to do all the work of finding the right friends and working through all the decisions of personal relationships, so we help them find playmates; and when they get into arguments and fights, we help them resolve them.
- We do not want them to have to make difficult

decisions about pleasurable yet dangerous temptations, so, for example, we do not allow them to take drugs.
- We do not want them to take on physical challenges for which they are not prepared, so we do not let them do unsupervised swimming, mountain climbing, or spelunking.

Protection is not the only parenting task, however. We all know what happens to overprotected children: they either become extraordinarily timid adults, never trying anything that the life of adulthood places in their path, or they make unusually bad decisions when faced with life's close calls. They end up isolated or incarcerated.

To avoid their isolation or incarceration, we must do more than protect our children, because protection has three limits. The first is pragmatic: We cannot hope to protect our children from everything that comes their way. The world is simply too large and complicated for that. The second is managerial: We do not want to have to protect them all their lives; in fact, we cannot, because sooner or later we are likely to precede them in death. The third is theological: Adult human beings have as one of their created purposes the freedom of choice. Children must therefore be taught to decide things for themselves.

To help our children achieve this created purpose, we must accomplish the second task of parenting, preparation. We prepare our children to slowly take over the task of protecting themselves. As they grow older they develop the powers of thinking, deciding, and discerning. Good parents encourage the growth of those powers by allowing their children to make some decisions themselves, to be exposed to the vicissitudes of life in increasingly complex doses. The art of parenting is to know just how much of that decision-making process should be turned over to children at different ages.

Different children are ready for different levels of responsibility at different ages. The great Swiss psychologist Paul Tournier once told me that he let his daughter make decisions at age eleven that he was not letting his son make at age seventeen. They matured at very different rates.

It might be more accurate to say that the art is knowing the timing of reversing the overall process: younger children need heavy doses of protection, so the parent's role reflects that—say, 90 percent protection, 10 percent preparation. As children grow older, those percentages reverse themselves to perhaps 10 percent protection and 90 percent preparation.

To use our examples above, older children begin to provide for their own physical needs (clothes, for example) and to make difficult social decisions (who to date, what friends to keep, who to avoid); and while we may worry about their mountaineering expedition, we also realize that it is up to them to choose what risks to take in life.

The Spiritual Component of Parenting

The spiritual dimension of parenting has similar dynamics. In the early years we protect our children fairly heavily from what we see as spiritual traps, but we never lose sight of the fact that the goal is to prepare them to make spiritual decisions for themselves as soon as they are able. In the spiritual dimension as in the more general task, some children become independent of parental protection much earlier than others.

Several factors influence how each parent carries out the task of preparation. First, how do you see your faith transmitted? For some, faith is mainly assent to a series of truth statements about God's nature and activity in the world. To transmit the knowledge of these statements, catechisms and creeds are drawn up and taught to children much like they are taught the facts of history and geography. For others, faith is getting in touch with the sense of God that we all have as part of our nature as a result of being God's created beings. Still others see faith as a series of actions, sometimes described as good deeds. To train children in the faith is to teach them to perform these actions regularly. Most of us view faith as a combination of all three of these things. How you emphasize the different elements makes a difference in how you make spiritual decisions for your children and prepare them for adulthood.

A second factor, one we have already mentioned, is the spiritual maturity of the child. Spiritual growth sometimes appears to have stages or levels of growth similar to physical and psychological growth. In a metaphorical sense, it is sometimes helpful to view faith development in this way, but it would be incorrect to think that the essence of faith is a developmental process. Faith is not an inevitable, invariant process of "growing up." In the Christian tradition it is a conscious acknowledgment of God's loving grace. It is assent to the truth of God's active grace, but it is also a trust that grace is a gift given to us to solve the dilemma of sin.

This understanding of faith makes the tasks of parenting even more difficult. It means that the range of spiritual maturity in children can vary even more widely than their physical and psychological development, which in turn makes the close calls of parenting more frequent and less sure.

A third factor in this decision-making process is the nature of the spiritual contacts being considered. These can range from simply knowing about what Jews, Hindus, Muslims, and Buddhists believe, to actually going to temples and mosques to observe or participate in worship services. It can mean playing with a neighborhood child or reading the sacred texts of that religion. It can mean going to a bar mitzvah as an observer or attending a two-week summer camp that teaches the basic beliefs of Hinduism. Unless you take one of the two polar opposite positions on this question—trying to eliminate all contact or allowing any and all contact—the nature of the contact being considered is very important.

David, Jordan, and Amitav

Even if the above delineation of parenting tasks and dimensions covered all the bases perfectly, which of course it does not, the decisions are still far from easy. Judy and I have discussed our parenting strategy upon occasion, and we do not always agree. We have even disagreed on the very topic of discussion—how much our children should be exposed to the beliefs and practices of non-Christian religions.

As a scholar of religion I visit many different places of worship and ritual of non-Christian religions. I enjoy taking the eldest of our sons on these trips. It is a way of spending time with him; selfishly, it relieves the tedium of being out in the field. Over the years I have taken David, for example, to a Nicheren Shoshu chanting service and a Louis Farrakan Nation of Islam rally. Judy has agreed to these trips but sometimes admits that she probably would feel more comfortable if we did not take them.

I have considered these trips to be safe educational experiences for David. What we see always generates questions that we discuss over a dish of ice cream later. Those discussions always involve comparisons with what we believe about the things we saw at the service and how those beliefs differ in both style and substance.

I have always taken thirteen-year-old David and never eleven-year-old Paul. At his age, I think Paul would be attracted in the wrong way to what goes on at some of these places. Paul and I go to baseball games instead. In fact, I think I would take nine-year-old Joe to the temples before I would Paul. My judgment of their relative powers of discernment, at least at this stage, forces me to make different decisions for the different children.

Judy and I believe that the process of transmitting faith is one of teaching content and encouraging assent to a "creed." However, we also believe that that wisdom must be seen in the context of our personal God-search, the nature of community worship, and how our beliefs fit into the overall patterns of belief and unbelief in the world. In our judgment, for David to visit a bar mitzvah and a sacred thread ceremony can only increase his ability to place the content of his developing faith in the context of personal faith, a worshiping community, and a religiously plural world. If we do not help David (and Paul and Joe) do that, we will have failed in preparing them for the kind of world in which we all live.

Yet that does not mean that we advocate David simply sampling every religious experience that comes down the pike. Since we do not think worship services are interchangeable between Christian and non-Christian meeting places, we would not encourage David to involve himself as a participant in any and all religious practices. Therefore, before letting him go, we must teach him the difference between being a participant and a respectful observer.

We also remind David that being a Christian means that each one of us represents the Christian church. As a representative of this faith, we must always be careful to let the light of Christ's love shine through everything we do. A good question to ask oneself in evaluating a potential interreligious experience is, *How can I be both respectful of my friend's beliefs and still a witness to my own faith?* Right now David would need guidance in asking and answering that question, so we must do heavy coaching, more protection than will later be necessary.

With these cautions and preparations, Judy and I decided that having David share these important religious milestones with his friends had far more upsides than downsides: he would learn about Judaism and Hinduism; in conversation with us afterward, the experience would deepen his understanding of Christianity; he would learn a little bit more about the religious complexity of the world; and he would be that much more confident about interreligious contacts in the future, contacts that are mandatory in our day for both evangelistic and humanitarian reasons.

The Question No One (or Everyone) Asks

In 1988 a couple walked into the office of the University Faith Council of a large Midwestern liberal arts college. It was two days before Christmas. Neither were students at the college, and they did not know the ministers who ran the council's ministry and worship program, but they wanted to get married. Denise, who was a Christian, wanted to get married in a Christian wedding ceremony. Denise and Rahul had asked several other Christian ministers to marry them, but all had declined. One problem was the timing: Rahul was a serviceman who would be shipped out to the Middle East on December 28. This left no time for the pastors to go through their mandatory three-to-six-session premarital counseling program. However, for most of the ministers they had asked, the lack of counseling opportunity was not the only problem. Rahul was not a Christian; he was a Muslim, and so far no minister asked was willing to perform an interfaith wedding.

Whenever interfaith relations in the neighborhoods of America are discussed, sooner or later the question of interfaith marriage comes up. Parents who have little problem with other aspects of interfaith interaction, such as educational programs about world religions, working together on projects of common social concern, or loving non-Christian neighbors, often draw the line at the prospect of their children marrying outside the Christian faith.

Sometimes they use the interfaith marriage danger as the sole reason for strictly or totally limiting other interfaith contacts. "I do not think it is wrong for my children to play with non-Christian kids," one parent told me. "But if we allow our children to play with non-Christians, we are dramatically increasing the chances that they will someday marry a person outside the faith."

Interfaith contacts do increase the number of interfaith marriages. Statistics about interfaith marriages in the United States are alarming to those who wish for their sons and daughters to marry within the faith. In a recent survey, 33 percent of all marriages in which at least one person was Jewish were interfaith marriages. Muslims in America struggle with similar statistics. Although Christian marriages, because of the demographics of this country, do not face those kinds of numbers, the question of interfaith marriages is a growing one. According to a survey reported in *Psychology Today*, in 1957 6 percent of Americans had a spouse of a different faith. Today that number has climbed to 17 percent of Protestants, 38 percent of Catholics, and 22 percent of Jews.[1]

For the vast majority of Christians, the question is not one of whether or not Christians should marry someone who is not a Christian. Almost any theology of marriage, historic or modern, advocates the model of both partners in a Christian marriage being Christian. Pastors, churches, and individual parents are often faced with whether or not to perform, sanction, or bless interfaith marriages. Although they come up with a variety of answers to that question, few argue against the ideal being for both partners to be committed to the Gospel of Jesus Christ. The Christian home they establish is then the incubator for nurturing Christian children, the future of the Christian church.

The question is really more one of how to best achieve the goal of having Christian homes. Does strictly limiting the contacts our children have with non-Christians lead to more marriages where both partners are Christian? Or does a freer policy of engagement somehow lead to a greater percentage of Christian marriages?

There is probably no way to answer this question in any kind of final sense, but several observations should be made, observations that would be helpful to parents who come down on both sides of the question.

First, it is very difficult to insure that children are not exposed to the members of non-Christian religions and their ideas. The example we used earlier of my son David and his friends at school indicates the trends toward pluralism that are greatly increasing the chances of our young people meeting, studying with, playing with, and working with young people of non-Christian faiths.

Second, even if it were possible to isolate them up to a certain age—marriageable age, for example—one could legitimately ask whether or not this kind of a parenting policy is the best for our day. Are we doing the best job of preparing our children to live in a pluralistic religious climate if we do not expose them to non-Christian ideologies—and non-Christian people?

Third, does limiting contacts really serve to increase the chances of our children marrying Christians? Parents are forever amazed at the wisdom of their children—if they are open to looking for it. Is it possible that our children have far greater powers of discernment than we give them credit for, at least by the time they are reaching marriageable age? Should we not consider the option of educating our children about the positive theology of marriage that is universal to Christian orthodoxy and trust them to act on it, rather than risk their negative backlash against what they might perceive as an overly restrictive contact policy?

Fourth, does limiting contacts hurt the evangelistic potential of our young people? With all the evangelistic emphasis on lifestyle witness and the importance of interpersonal relationships in the evangelistic task, what does a strict policy of separation do to the obligation of the Great Commission? Does it not sharply restrict us to certain proclamation methods of evangelism? Although such types of evangelism are important, strategy studies have shown that they need to be augmented with interpersonal, lifestyle methods.

I know that talking about evangelism in the same breath I use to talk about the marriage of my child may seem crass. I have heard young people in love talk about the potential for mission in an interfaith relationship: "I'll make him a Christian, Dad." And I have heard pastors talk about the mission aspect of a church having as open a marriage policy as possible. But I have never heard parents use the argument, especially when their son or daughter is concerned. There is probably no area of parenting where the balance between the protection and preparation aspect of the task is trickier.

I would not propose the argument in a primary sense; I suspect that the number of non-Christian marriage partners who change their faith after marriage is small. In a secondary sense, however, the evangelistic question can be raised. What are we modeling to our young people when we strictly limit contacts with non-Christian young people? That they are dangerous characters? That our faith is not strong enough to stand up to such contact? That we have more of a responsibility to protect our own faith than to tell others about it? All of these attitudes are suspect. They hurt the witness of the church, and, in the long run, probably do not produce the very effects we seek.

8

Is It All Right to Worship with People of Other Faiths?

"Hear, O my people, and I will warn you—
    if you would but listen to me, O Israel!
You shall have no foreign god among you;
    you shall not bow down to an alien god.
I am the LORD your God."

(Ps. 81:8–10)

Not only do we have difficult decisions to make about the kind of contact our children have with those of other faiths; we must also make choices for ourselves. One of the most common choices we are called to make is whether or not to worship with non-Christians.

It usually comes about in a manner similar to this scenario: We slowly became acquainted with our neighbors. They received our mail a couple of times by mistake and brought it over. When our lawn mower broke, we borrowed theirs. Once their car broke down, and they asked if we could drop off their kids at school along with ours. Over time a warm speaking relationship developed. Last summer it culminated in our inviting them to a Labor Day lunch of cold cuts.

We had such a good time over roast beef and rye that we decided to invite them to church. They are Muslim, but they accepted our invitation. They were gracious during the visit but seemed satisfied with their own faith, and our gentle prodding led to no further questions on their part. Then, a month after their visit to our church, they invited us to the mosque—and to a basement supper afterward for their annual celebration of Abraham's great obedience in being willing to offer his son (Ishmael, not Isaac, for Muslims) to God at God's request.

Should we go?

If this were simply a matter of common courtesy, the answer would be obvious. They accepted our invitation to attend worship at the Christian church, so we should be willing to accept their invitation to worship at the mosque. Quid pro quo. However, because worship is such a central, intimate spiritual act, and because the Bible has some pretty clear things to say about the subject, this matter should not be merely reciprocating hospitality. It should be thought through as a serious theological question. Neighborliness should be a factor in the decision, but it must take a backseat to theological considerations.

When we look at the question theologically, we discover that the question changes its form slightly, depending on what our neighbors' expectations are of our presence at the mosque. An analogy might be the question of whether a girl should go out with a boy when he asks her. If his invitation is for a movie and ice cream only, the answer may be yes. If the expectation he holds for the girl's agreeing to go, however, is marriage, then a lot more thinking needs to be done before assent it given. Whether or not we go to the mosque depends on what our neighbors expect. Expectations that *may* reside in our neighbor's request can be lumped into three categories.

1. A visit to observe worship. Most invitations will be of this simple variety. Your friends simply want to show you what they do at the mosque. Because their faith means a lot to them, they want to share it with you by showing how they pray to Allah and honor the prophet Muhammad.

The prayer service will probably be on Friday at noon, when Muslims worldwide gather for prayers at mosques.

Upon entering the mosque, you will be asked to take off your shoes as a sign of respect for their meeting place. You can sit at the back of the hall to observe the proceedings. In most mosques women meet separately from the men, sometimes in a different part of the same room, sometimes in a different room altogether.

There may be some sharing of beliefs on a personal level; it is more likely, however, that the only expectation of you is that you be properly reverent and honor their customs. Just as we would expect them to be properly respectful in our church, so we should observe decorum in theirs.

This all seems innocuous enough. What possible objection could we have to this kind of visit to another place of worship?

Objections might take two forms. First, some might feel that visiting another place of worship gives succor to the "enemy." That is, simply by being on their home turf we endorse what goes on there.

One of the assumptions behind this kind of objection—that those of other religions are enemies—is problematic for many of us. There are better ways of looking at people of other religions. Even if we grant for argument's sake that they are opponents of some kind (see chapter 3), to avoid them for that reason is contradicted by our fundamental assumption that the command to love one's neighbor is unconditional. In fact, Christ extended the command to love enemies as well as neighbors. Further, although we might consider some non-Christian *ideas* to be "enemies" to be fought, the clear intent of Scripture is to love other *people* unconditionally.

Second, some might think that there is something holy (or unholy) about the physical place of worship of another religion. For many religions the place of worship is inherently holy. In our own history, for example, some places in the Hebrew temple were so holy that only certain people at certain times of the year could enter them.

Over time, "holy places" changed in the Christian tradition. Jesus told the woman at the well that the Gospel he brought was a gospel of spirit and truth, not of physical places and holy shrines (John 4:19–24). As Christians we should have no qualms about holy places. Our rock is built on holy ideas, specifically the mighty, holy acts of God in history.

Since Muslims are not our enemies and holiness is not a physical place, as long as the expectations of us at the mosque are to observe their worship respectfully and nothing more, we should not hesitate to accept our friend's invitation to visit.

2. *Participation in mutual worship.* Sometimes the expectation of such a visit is more, however. Sometimes the expectation is for mutual worship. For example, our friends might be thinking that when we visit the mosque, we can use the Muslim worship forms to worship the God of Abraham, Isaac, and Jacob. While our friends are offering prayers of praise to Allah (the God of Abraham and Ishmael), we can offer prayers of praise to God. Can we?

Last year a student of mine told me the story of Stephen and Sheila, who worshiped at her church. This young couple met at college, fell in love, and married. He is Christian and she is Jewish. Today they worship in and belong to a Methodist church, but she has, by her own understandings, remained Jewish. Because the pastor of this Methodist church believes that Jews do not need to be Christianized and that God's covenant with them was not superseded by the life of Jesus Christ, he is particularly sensitive to Sheila's heritage in his sermons and worship forms, and she feels comfortable worshiping at this church.

Is it possible for Christians to feel similarly comfortable worshiping God in a mosque, knowing that the people around us understand the worship setting and forms in a distinctly different way from what we do?

The key question for us to consider in such a scenario is how we understand the jealousy of God. Is God a jealous God, and if so, how are we to understand this jealousy? What does Exodus 34:14 mean when it says, "Do not worship any other god, for the LORD, whose name is Jealous, is a jealous God"?

And what sort of provocation is Paul talking about in 1 Corinthians 10:21–22: "You cannot drink the cup of the Lord and the cup of demons too; you cannot have a part in both the Lord's table and the table of demons. Are we trying to arouse the Lord's jealousy? Are we stronger than he?"

A study of how the word *jealousy* as used in the New Testament indicates that mere physical proximity to "other gods" is not enough to provoke God's jealousy. In 1 Corinthians 10, Paul says that what does provoke the Lord to jealousy is actually worshiping other gods, and he uses several incidents from Israel's history as examples. He is warning the Corinthians not to fall into the same trap.

One interpretation of this might be that (1) as long as you are very clear in your own mind about who it is you are worshiping in the mosque, and (2) you clearly know the difference between that and the understandings of the others in that place, and (3) you can freely make appropriate mental allowances in the worship forms being used so that they are consistent with your understandings of who God is and what God requires in worship, then mutual worship might be possible.

Another interpretation—one that is a bit more restrictive in its understandings about just what it is that provokes God's jealousy—would say that mutual worship is actually impossible, or at least so difficult that it is impractical. If mutual worship is what is expected in your friend's invitation, you would do better to graciously decline, explaining that this is not meant to be disrespectful but is simply a position that your religious beliefs require you to take.

3. A common worship service. The third possible expectation depends on ideological pluralism—that all the religions are different paths to the same ultimate reality—for its rationale. Ideological pluralism, remember, believes that although the different religions have distinctive practices and beliefs, at the core they are all the same. The worship patterns, rituals, and practices of personal piety are the culturally determined forms the universal human quest for God takes.

If ideological pluralism underlies a worship setting, the different forms of worship take on an optional cast. One is as good as another, and since the ultimate reality to whom all worship is directed is the same, you can invest whatever meaning you want into each. In effect, they are interchangeable.

In this view, worship practices are like the different languages of the world. The languages all communicate basically the same information—human feelings, facts, and observations—but different words are used. One can learn one, two, or more languages and use them interchangeably, depending on the location and purpose of the language.

Although this position has been written about extensively in the past two decades, it is the position held by a minority of religious people. Most religious people in the world, whether Christian, Muslim, Hindu, Buddhist, or Jewish, believe their religion is uniquely distinct from the others.

If this is the expectation underlying the invitation to worship in another setting, the key question for us to answer is simple: Is there any ultimate difference between Christianity and the other religions?

Levels of Cooperation

Whether or not to worship with those of non-Christian religions is an important question about interfaith relationships, but it is not the only one. Deciding questions about permissible contact can be difficult if done solely on a case by case basis. It is helpful to have an underlying idea of what kind of contact in general we endorse. Knowing the range of possibilities for what kind of relationships other groups have with different religions will help us find our place. Let us consider a spectrum that has at the one end active hostility and at the other end total identification.

1. Active hostility. Religions that are actively hostile toward others usually do not last long. If they do last, they usually remain small. Unless they are tied to political power of significant proportion, hostile religions burn themselves out on their own hate.

Hostile religions generally fall into two categories: cults and antireligions. The classic example of an actively hostile cult in recent times is the People's Temple of Jim Jones. The paranoia and hate that drove them to the jungles of Guiana eventually also drove them to mass suicide. Unrestricted hate and separation as an ideological cornerstone ultimately creates emotions that are too powerful to control. Increasingly fine distinctions between the "saved" and the "unsaved," combined with a total disregard for the rights of the unsaved, make this kind of religion extremely unstable, unable to live with any kind of political or societal structure, even of its own forms.

The classic modern antireligion of this type is certain forms of Marxism. The collapse of Marxist systems that are hostilely antireligious has become almost a cliche in the past decade. Hostile antireligions often last a bit longer than hostile cults because they usually enjoy political power which can be used to force their ideology on the masses, but eventually the universal religious urge of human beings comes to the fore and the antireligion fades into history.

2. Passive hostility. A longer lasting version of the hostile position is the passively hostile one. In these religions the hostility takes different forms: sometimes passionate hate rhetoric is used to inspire the followers, but the rhetoric is never followed up with visible demonstrations of hostility. The hate rhetoric is understood to be just that: rhetoric used to hold the group together in their common dislike for other religions. But no one, pastor or people, really expects the hate to be physically acted on.

Christian churches in the United States have often taken this stance toward the pagan churches of the world. Sometimes it is easier to rally support for missions programs if the element of fighting the evil, heathen forces of the world is used. War imagery is common and usually effective.

This kind of position is easier to take when the people talked about are personally unknown to members of the congregation. It is much easier to talk negatively about people and their beliefs when we do not know them personally. If we do get to know them personally and find that they are sincere, decent folks just like us, then the passively hostile position is more difficult to maintain.

3. *Peaceful coexistence.* The passively hostile position is thus often replaced with that of peaceful coexistence. In the United States, as religious pluralism has grown and as we have become acquainted with our neighbors, peaceful coexistence has often replaced passive hostility as the attitude of choice.

Peaceful coexistence is especially useful when we all recognize that the laws of religious freedom in this country demand that these other people have a right to worship as they please. The freedoms we enjoy have to be extended to others or we are in danger of losing them ourselves.

It is possible, indeed common, to adopt the peaceful coexistence attitude and still hold to various degrees of separation. Peaceful coexistence does not require any more contact than is necessary. We do not have to get to know people of other religions or learn about their beliefs, and we certainly do not have to visit their places of worship. However, we do acknowledge their right to exist and practice their religion.

4. *Mutual respect.* This position not only accepts people of other religions as valid neighbors; it grants them respect because some element of their system or practice strikes a positive chord with us. It may be the sincerity with which they practice their religion, the fruits of what they do (the way their children behave, the social works they support), or even

some aspect of their belief system that seems particularly attractive.

Mutual respect does not mean that we agree with this other religion or that we think it is true (at least not all of it). But it does mean that we value what they are doing and the way they are doing it.

5. *Cooperation.* We not only respect what other religions do, but we want to work together with them on tasks of common concern: feeding the hungry, caring for orphans, and supplying medicines and medical help for the sick. This does not necessarily mean that we agree with the basic beliefs and practices of the other religion, although we may agree with some elements.

It does mean that we agree with the basic sincerity and goodness of what they are doing and that we are willing to put our reputation on the line in working with them in public causes. This usually implies several things: that we are convinced the project is worthwhile, that acceptable means will be used to achieve it, and that the people we are working with have a basic respect for us that matches our respect for them.

6. *Intercommunion.* So far on our spectrum, all of the positions are extrachurch. There are no common worship services and no question of sharing beliefs or formal rituals. Intercommunion raises the possibility that there are certain religious practices on which we have common ground, so we can share them. In ecumenical Christian circles, the most basic of these commonalities are baptism, the Eucharist (Communion), and the ministry functions essential in delivering these sacraments.

The concept can be extended to other religions, however. It implies a recognition of some kind of universal human religious urge. We all seek some kind of "god," so let us do that seeking together, even though we may disagree on what the seeking entails.

In interreligious situations, the most common form that intercommunion takes is sharing in life transitional services: births, marriages, and funerals. Leaders of the different religions do different things in these services where somehow both religions are represented in the families involved. This may also include common Thanksgiving services with those of other religious traditions.

7. Ideological unity I (core doctrines). A rarer form of cooperation is to identify a core of doctrines common to all. Some religions, such as the Bahai, have attempted to do this on a large scale, showing how all the major religious teachers of the world taught very similar things. We should not let the differences in our religious traditions stand in the way of affirming the commonalities of their doctrines.

Members of such churches feel free to study the teachings of all the major religions, or just one or two, but they focus on the core teachings that all affirm in the public practice of their faith. In many of these kinds of churches the focus of common concern tends to be on the peace-seeking and humanitarian elements of all religions.

8. Ideological unity II (all doctrines). Attempts are made to bring all doctrines together, usually by searching for some underlying abstraction that unifies them. Thus baptism in Christianity is seen as a community bonding ceremony, matched by a quite different ceremony in a different religion, but one with the same intent.

In such systems, the content of beliefs and rituals often takes a back seat to their symbolic importance. If beliefs and doctrines are increasingly pushed to higher and higher levels of abstraction, common denominators are eventually found and considered central to belief.

9. Structural unity. Once doctrinal agreement is found, some kind of overall structural unity may be desired. At first this may mean simply an umbrella group, membership in which shows basic agreement on all the essentials of faith but a desire to still maintain some kind of separate identity for any one of several purposes: ecclesiological, ethnic, cultural, or political. This kind of structure is still theoretical today, although some small religious umbrella groups are trying to claim this status.

10. Identification. Some religious groups (the Universalist Unitarians come to mind) attempt to create a belief system that incorporates the common core of all religions so that a one-world "theology" is achieved. A new synthesis is brought out of the historical particularity of all the religions and becomes a new religion in itself. This system requires a commitment to a common structure as well as a belief system. Unity becomes a tenet of faith.

Interestingly, some of these kinds of groups actually come full circle and create a new particularity, a commitment to one absolute, right religion out of a commitment to include everything in the world's religions. Sometimes this can congeal into an attitude of exclusiveness, of religiously correct thinking that shuts out all other, "lesser," systems. Much depends on the attitude taken by such a group. It can become hostile toward other groups and in a sense turn our linear spectrum into a circle.

Deciding where you fall on this spectrum forces clearer definitions of loving neighbors and preaching truth. It would seem that the command to love neighbors would preclude the hostile positions and that preaching truth would preclude the relativist positions that view theology as optional or as simply a matter of taste.

Preaching truth also demands a clear definition of truth. Truth is defined in orthodox Christianity as that which is proclaimed in the biblical story. This historical specificity makes the positions on the higher end of the spectrum difficult to justify. If the story of Jesus is seen as definitive, then the story of the Buddha can be seen as important, instructive, and interesting, but necessarily on a lower level than that of Jesus.

Once the uniqueness of Jesus is accepted, we are left deciding between the middle positions on our spectrum. Deciding between those positions often depends largely on questions of evangelism: the methods of evangelism, the nature of the people being evangelized, and the effectiveness of evangelism. To those questions we now turn.

Part 3
Sharing Faith

ALL RELIGIONS DEAL WITH THE FATE OF SOULS, YET not all religious people agree on just what role each of us play in the fate of our neighbor's soul. Traditional Christianity has always contended that sharing our faith with our neighbor has something to do with the fate of our neighbor's soul. But the consensus stops there. Christians disagree on many things about sharing faith. What is our actual responsibility? Does the fate of my neighbor really hinge on how good an evangelist I am? Three images of evangelism characterize the different views we have of it:

The war image. We must win the world for Christ, and in this battle there will be casualties. The casualties of this war are those who will not fight; the spoils of this war are the souls of our non-Christian neighbors.

The competition image. Like it or not, we are in a competition with other religions for the souls of our neighbors. Most games have rules; what are the rules for the competition of souls? Do we make them up? Which is more important, following the rules or winning the game?

The unity of humankind image. We are all just struggling in our search to find God. Rather than tell one another the right way to struggle, let us support each other however we can.

Deciding between these images demands that we answer for ourselves the questions of the following three chapters.

9

Are My Non-Christian Neighbors Going to Hell?

SEVERAL YEARS AGO I WAS ON A RADIO TALK SHOW. The host was Chicago's Milt Rosenberg, one of the best. The show was a discussion of televangelist Pat Robertson's run for the presidency. I was representing the evangelical voice of sympathetic reason, perched comfortably between the fundamentalist advocate for Robertson's run and the liberal proponent, a former *PTL* employee who had just sketched out in a book the dire consequences that might eventuate if Robertson were president: reliance on "words of knowledge" for major political decisions, a witch-hunt for non-Christian liberals, and various and sundry mistakes born of general political inexperience.

Suddenly, Rosenberg, who describes himself as an agnostic Jew, turned to me and said, "Terry, let's assume that I am never going to believe the Good News of Jesus Christ. Do you think I am going to hell?"

Even though I had come prepared for such a question (friends told me it was one of Rosenberg's favorites for evangelicals—he had sprung it on Charles Colson two months previous), the force of it was startling. It is difficult to look someone in the eye and tell him that he is going to hell. For that reason, people who believe that the Bible teaches some kind of eternal punishment for those who do not accept the

Gospel are often reluctant to preach it or even talk about it. Rosenberg had tried to put me in that position.

In Rosenberg's case, of course, the intent of the question was to paint conservative Christians as wild-eyed fanatics, triumphalist to the point of glee over lost souls. Since this idea is built on a misunderstanding of the biblical position, ascribing judgment to human beings instead of to God, it is easily dealt with. (For the gist of how I answered Rosenberg, see "Muck's Maxims" at the end of this chapter.)

It is harder to deal with more immediate, personal forms of the question. A teary-eyed older woman came up to me one Sunday after a class I was teaching on whether non-Christians are saved: "Dr. Muck, your remarks made me think of a question. My Uncle Dick. We told him and told him the Gospel story when he was alive, but as far as we know, he never made a decision for Jesus Christ. In fact, he was very negative toward the church. Do you think he's in hell?"

Even though I said that this book would deal mainly with questions that fall somewhere between the bookend issues of creation and salvation, the question of salvation almost always intrudes on any Christian discussion of other religions. Can non-Christians be saved?

The question is certainly one that theologians want to ask, and they need to. Salvation, after all, is the heart and soul of Christian doctrine and experience. But the question, as we have seen, has its unscholarly form as well.

I was teaching a Sunday school class on religious pluralism in America. We had talked about the growing numbers of non-Christian religions in America and what this meant for us in terms of loving our neighbors and of interchurch/mosque/temple relationships. A young woman came up after class and posed the theological question: "I'm a student at the University of Texas," she said. "I have gotten to know two Thai students very well. They're Buddhist. We have many of the same classes. They're kind and smart, and as near as I can tell, good people. We've become good friends. Are they going to hell?"

Questions about what role other religions play in the salvation process are not foreign to the history of Christianity. New Testament Christians faced the wrenching decisions about what role Judaism played in the revelation of Jesus Christ. Paul warned his fledgling flocks against Eastern mystery religions, Gnosticism, and emperor worship. Augustine, perhaps the greatest of the church's theologians, tried Manicheanism, an early dualistic religion. Aquinas wrote a five-volume work, *Summa Contra Gentiles*, about missions in Africa. Luther screamed about the Muslim Turks, and Barth warned about over-accommodating comparisons with Amida Buddhism.

Although the experience of other religions has been a common feature throughout history, the answers about what role they play in salvation has not been common. Many different viewpoints have emerged, some avowing that the other religions play no positive part in Christian salvation, others hinting at limited involvement, and some suggesting that salvation is possible for members of all religions.

The reason for the conflicting viewpoints can, in part at least, be traced to two teachings in the New Testament, teachings that in some ways seem to conflict with one another. The first of these teachings deals with *God's requirements* for salvation: the only way to salvation is through Jesus Christ (cf. Acts 4:12). John's gospel speaks clearly of Jesus' self-understanding that he was God's chosen way of salvation: "I am the way and the truth and the life. No one comes to the Father except through me" (14:6). The apostle Paul often told his far-flung churches that their only hope was in Jesus Christ (for example, Eph. 1:12; Col. 1:27; 1 Tim. 1:1).

A second biblical teaching, however, emphasizes *God's mercy*: it states that God strongly desires that everyone be saved. Statements in Romans and 1 Timothy clearly express this divine desire: "For God has bound all men over to disobedience so that he may have mercy on them all" (Rom. 11:32); "God our Savior . . . wants all men to be saved and to come to a knowledge of the truth" (1 Tim. 2:3–4).

If understood in one way, these two teachings need not conflict. If God is limited in power, then even though God desires the salvation of all, God is, for one reason or another, unable to pull it off: either God set up a world where he was limited in this one respect (the free will of human beings) or else he is really limited in power.

If God is truly all-powerful and sovereign (not only powerful but using the power in an ongoing way), however, then this expressed desire to save all humankind does indeed bump up against the teaching that Jesus Christ is the only gate through which the unredeemed may pass. If an all-powerful God wants it, then an all-powerful God will get it.

Throughout Christian history, theologians and philosophers have devised different solutions to this difficulty. Their positions can be summarized under one of five answers to the question, "Who will be saved?"

Answer #1: "All Human Beings Will Be Saved."

Sometimes this position has been called universalism. When used in this context, universalism implies two things. First, it heavily emphasizes the second of our two New Testament axioms, that God desires all human beings be saved. Second, it strongly affirms the power of God: if God desires all to be saved, then God will make this desire a reality. All will be saved; salvation will be universal.

Universalists do not always agree on how God will accomplish this. Some have quite specific scenarios, others say we cannot know the how. But on the fact of universal salvation they agree.

Universalists have a long history in the church. One of the first to articulate the position was Origen, who used the term *apokatastasis* to teach this wide application of God's mercy. Other early universalists were Clement of Alexandria and Gregory of Nyssa.

Modern universalism can probably best be traced to Friedrich Schleiermacher, an eighteenth-century European philosopher who located the essence of religion not in external revelations (such as the Bible), religious rites (worship and the sacraments), or teachings (creeds or doctrine), but in the feeling of absolute dependence each of us has for a higher power. This feeling, Schleiermacher maintained, is universal, but the form it takes varies from religion to religion, culture to culture, even person to person. We should not worry about the form religion takes; religion's true task is to provide a satisfying outlet for this feeling. Form follows feeling. The personal supersedes the communal.

Perhaps the most articulate of the modern writers in this universalist tradition is Wilfred Cantwell Smith. In *The Meaning and End of Religion*, Smith argues that since all religious traditions can be shown to rely heavily on culture and historical change, none can be considered propositionally true. The "essence" must be that they all represent humankind's never-ending quest for God.[1]

Universalists give voice to the discomfort we all feel with the idea that any of our fellow human beings might be subjected to eternal punishment. It solves part of the problem of the existence of evil by assuring any and all that God prevails over evil, especially in this most crucial area of individual quest for salvation.

Universalism appeals particularly to a shrinking world where it is becoming increasingly obvious that the skills needed for the future must include heavy doses of Christian love and acceptance. Put in simple terms, in the past eras of relative religious homogeneity (usually enforced by cultural and political fiat) and the relative separation of Christian groups by distance and time, it was somewhat easy to consign unknown non-Christians to eternal punishment. It is much harder, however, to think the same about one's neighbor, to tell a counselee the implications of unrepentant sin, or to compound political and economic imperialism with what seems to be religious imperialism.

If we were all free to choose which answer we want to the question *Who will be saved?* universalism would surely win the most votes. From our perspective, it certainly seems the most humane. There are other factors, however, besides what we would like.

Answer #2: "All Sincere Religious Seekers Will Be Saved."

This position is sometimes called pluralism. Pluralists emphasize the same truths as universalists emphasize but with one addition. The addition implies that some kind of *religious seeking* is required for "salvation."

Pluralists are less concerned with the form of the religious seeker's path than with the fact that sincere seeking takes place. Whether the path be Hinduism, Buddhism, Islam, or New Ageism is not as important as the diligence with which the Hindu, Buddhist, Muslim, or Aquarian seeks. Pluralism does not care about the label as much as the lived life.

Pluralism has gained adherents in religiously plural situations. As religious freedom and increasing immigration have turned the formerly Protestant United States into a religious cornucopia, we have become increasingly perplexed about how to think about the Muslims, Buddhists, and Hindus we meet in our neighborhoods and at work—they are ethical and sincere. Surely they are in a different class than the run-of-the-mill sinners.

The reluctance to judge anyone a sinner has grown appreciably in our culture. For example, I was teaching a world religions class at the University of Texas. Although I usually do not teach the class this way, one day on a whim I said something like this: "Wow, there sure are a lot of religions around here. Should we try to figure out which one is the right one?"

It was as if I had thrown a lighted match into a gas tank. "We can't do that!" several flashed. "Who are we to judge other people's religions? We'll believe what each of us thinks is true and let others believe what they think is true. And we'll all be right." (Some added "more or less" to that last statement.)

As John Hick, professor of philosophy at Claremont Graduate School and the foremost modern pluralist, has said, we must cross a "theological Rubicon" and abandon "the conviction that outside Christianity there is no salvation," an absolutist position that Hick says "most thinking Christians have abandoned in the past seventy years."[2]

Universalism makes salvation inevitable; pluralism offers the franchise to any and all who are willing to seek and accept it. Universalists make salvation a part of being human, pluralists make it a part of being a good human.

Answer #3: "Because of What God Did Through Jesus Christ, All Sincere Religious Seekers Will Be Saved."

Some have attempted to solve the dilemma of God's mercy and God's requirements by loosening the requirements without doing away with them. In a nutshell, the classic requirements for Christian salvation are two: (1) that Jesus Christ did what he did (died on the cross for our sins), and (2) that people know about and somehow acknowledge that Jesus Christ did what he did.

One way to soften the second of these requirements, the acknowledgement of Christ's deed, is to broaden what it takes to make this acknowledgment. Suppose, they say, that we do not have to know exactly about the historical person called Jesus. We do not know that he lived in first-century Palestine, that he preached, and that he was arrested by Roman authorities and crucified. Suppose we do not know that he was raised from the dead and that he did all this to pay for the sins of humanity.

Suppose we do know the following: that something about this life we are living is wrong (our consciences tell us so). We know from observing the wonders of nature, the design behind creation, that there must be a God who created all this. And we know that the religious seeking that our Hindu (or whatever) family and friends are doing is well motivated and sincere; it is a genuine search for this same God that we recognize must be out there. So we make a response that such a wonderful God must deserve our allegiance and obedience.

Should not that qualify as satisfying the second of our requirements for salvation? Note some of the features of this position, which is usually called inclusivism.

1. It allows that a few people of other religions could be saved through this natural, nonspecific knowledge of God. The foremost modern exponent of this position, Roman Catholic theologian Karl Rahner, called these people "anonymous Christians."

2. What Jesus Christ did is still absolutely essential. If Christ had not died on the cross and rose from the dead, there would be no hope for any of us.

3. This would solve the fairness question often asked about the classical requirements for salvation—that is, what about people who just because of circumstances of birth and geography, never in their life hear the story of Jesus? Would it be fair to think of them consigned to eternal punishment through no fault of their own?

A growing number of theologians are taking this position because it maintains the uniqueness of Christianity as the only way to salvation, but it also allows the full expression of God's mercy. Proponents point to passages like Romans 1:18–20 and 2:14–15 that seem to allow for us to learn about God through nature and our consciences.

Answer #4: "Those Who Acknowledge God's Unique Work in Jesus Christ Will Be Saved."

Theologians who hold this position acknowledge along with the inclusivists that there is a common religious denominator that unifies all of humanity and makes the religious quest something all of us, both Christians and nonChristians, share. John Calvin called this common denominator the *sensus divinitatis.*

However, Calvin and his kin disagree with the inclusivists that the knowledge gained in this quest can ever lead to salvation unless explicit awareness of Jesus Christ and what he did becomes part of the knowledge. Salvation comes only to those who specifically know about Jesus. Because these theologians stick to the letter of the classic requirements for salvation, thereby eliminating from the company of the saved those who have never heard about the way of salvation, they are called exclusivists.

Exclusivism has historically been far and away the dominant position in Christianity, and it still is. Both in the past and today, the vast majority of theologians, clerics, and laypeople hold to some kind of exclusivist position. They point to biblical passages such as 1 Corinthians 3:10–17 ("No one can lay any foundation other than the one already laid, which is Jesus Christ" [v. 11]) and say that the uniqueness of Jesus Christ is final.

Because of this committed attitude toward what are certainly clear scriptural statements about Jesus Christ's uniqueness, exclusivists are dismissed by some modern theologians as unfeeling fanatics, religious Svengalis who care for little but their overly literalistic readings of the Bible. This is an unfair, inaccurate characterization. Many who take this position do so out of the highest regard for God's sovereignty and their feeble ability to understand what seems to be God's selective will. This is what God has said in Scripture, they say, and we must obey.

Some exclusivists point to more than Scripture to support their position. In arguing particularly against the inclusivist's position, they ask what would happen to the motivation for missions if we allowed that those in other religions might be saved? Why should we obey the Great Commission if Buddhism is as good as Christianity?

While maintaining a strict exclusivist stance, many have tried to answer the tougher questions that this position engenders. Almost all allow that children and the mentally incompetent are taken care of by God outside the exclusivist framework, for example. But there are other, tougher questions.

What about those who have never heard? Is it fair to judge them when they do not even have a chance? "Second-chance exclusivists" point to passages such as 1 Peter 3:19 and say that God gives those who die without hearing the Gospel story a second chance, usually by Jesus Christ going to wherever these disembodied souls are and preaching to them.

What about the biblical statements that say that God desires all to be saved? "Hope-so universalists" (they are really "hope-not exclusivists") say that we must behave as if we are exclusivists, preaching the unique Gospel of Jesus Christ to everyone because that is what Scripture clearly commands. But because we know that God is both all-loving and all-powerful, we must hope that somehow at the end of time all will indeed be saved. For now, however, we must behave as exclusivists.

Is it not arrogant to think we know who is saved and who is not? "Agnostic exclusivists" say that in principle, when talking about people as a group, the teachings of Scripture clearly support the exclusivist position. But when talking about individual people, none of us really knows who is going to be saved and who is not. So let us admit we do not really know this (be "agnostic" about this one aspect of the Christian life) and get on with our business of preaching the Gospel as best we can to all we can.

Answer #5: "No One Will Be Saved."

This is the naturalist's answer, one held by many in our secular world. At least many claim to hold it. It is typified by the television beer commercial that claims that "we only go around once in this world, and we need to grab for all the gusto we can." Naturalists would agree that this one life is all we have, and when we die that is the end.

This position has been articulated well by some philosophers (Bertrand Russell was one of the best), but is obviously an antireligion position that satisfies none of the deeper questions of life. It simply says that those are questions we need not even ask.

Sometimes the complexity of life makes us want to throw up our hands and toss in our lot with the naturalists. Usually we choose to struggle with the other four positions.

Muck's Maxims on Salvation

Regardless of what you decide in your struggle with the above positions on salvation, it is good to keep the following thoughts in mind:

1. Be cautious about judgment. As clear as the two teachings about God's mercy and God's requirements are, there is a third teaching in Scripture that is equally clear: "Do not judge, or you too will be judged" (Matt. 7:1).

2. Is "Who will be saved?" always the right question? In a theology class it might be. As a theoretical motivation for missions it probably is. But as Lesslie Newbigin has convincingly pointed out, there are many times when a much better question is, "How is God's grace working in this person's life?" and the follow-up question, "How can I best aid and abet that process?"[3]

3. The best question is, "How can God be glorified?" We must welcome all signs of God's grace in this world. That means that when we meet other people, instead of trying to determine whether or not they are going to hell, a better response, as we prepare to witness to them, is to look for the working of God in their lives.

10

How Should I Go About Sharing My Faith?

FOR CHRISTIANS, THE PRESENCE OF PEOPLE OF OTHER religions in our neighborhoods is more than a fact. It is something that calls for action—telling them the Gospel story. The command to do this is clear-cut in Scripture. The passage most often referred to in support of this is the Great Commission, found in Matthew 28:18–20, but many other New Testament passages witness to this obligation as well.

These New Testament passages also witness to an incredible variety of ways in which this obligation can be carried out. Sometimes it is public preaching, sometimes a private exchange of faith journeys. Sometimes it is a debate over the fine points of "theologies," sometimes nothing more than sharing "a cup of cold water." All these "methods" help accomplish the central task of communicating the story to those who have never heard.

The variety of methods can be confusing. Many incidents in which such communication takes place are obviously not planned; people meet, people talk, the Gospel is shared. Other times the use of certain methods does seem intentional. If one takes the time to plan the sharing of the Gospel with a neighbor, the natural question that arises is *How should I do it?* With a variety of scriptural models of different kinds of communication, how do I decide which to use in specific cases? Are some better than others? Are some illegitimate?

The Danger of Human Motivation

Sharing one's faith is never a simple matter. The complexity comes not just from a variety of methods from which to choose; it also comes from the variety of human motivations we bring to the task. Take the matter of our self-centeredness: too many self-oriented passions intrude on the process. At any moment, any one of these "self-isms" may predominate, turning a healthy exchange of the Gospel into a manipulative one. These powerful emotions include self-righteousness: wanting to be right in the eyes of others; self-protection: sheltering our sensitive egos; self-promotion: desiring control over other people; self-perspective: seeing life mainly from our own point of view.

These selfish human desires conflict with the selfless, charitable orientation of the Gospel. The Gospel teaches self-sacrifice and obedience, not self-aggrandizement and independence. If our human nature and the Gospel message did not conflict, we would not have a problem. We could carry out the New Testament command to share the Gospel with others and could also go about the business of self-centeredness. Unfortunately the two concepts do conflict and in the worst possible way.

Here is what I mean by the worst possible way. Some of life's conflicts are obvious: doing one thing well often implies we do another thing not so well. For example, becoming a really great trombone player means hours of practice. As a result, a great trombone player will probably not also become a great piano player. The time spent on the one decreases the amount of time spent on the other. We might call this type of conflict, where one thing precludes another, a simple conflict.

There are also conflicts in life where doing one thing well seems to help us do another thing well. But this compatibility turns out to be only a surface agreement. When we look at the subtle, underlying motives driving each action, we see that there is a conflict. For example, developing the virtue of charity, or giving to the poor, requires that a person practice selfless giving. Yet the tax laws in this country make giving to charitable causes something that helps us make more money—or more precisely, save money by having to pay less taxes. Instead of selflessness, charity turns out to be self-promoting. More money and more honor, rather than less, actually come to the giver. Since in most cases developing the virtue of charity demands anonymity and genuine sacrifice, most charitable giving in our culture actually works to defeat the very conditions needed to promote the true virtue of charity. Both goals (becoming charitable and aiding the poor) seem to be promoted, but in reality they work against one another. We might call this kind of conflict a complex conflict.

The relationship between sharing one's faith and growing in the faith can become a complex conflict. Christian faith can be shared, people can come to know Christ and become less the victims of injustice in this world, and the kingdom of God can be enhanced, while at the same time the selfish motives of individual sharers of the faith can also be increased.

Perhaps the best, although admittedly extreme, case to illustrate this phenomenon are the recent cases of Jim Bakker and some of the other televangelists. It is true that they proclaimed the Gospel on their television shows, making a significant difference in some viewers' lives. But their ministries as a whole had a negative influence on them by promoting their basest instincts of greed and extravagance.

Thus, asking the question "*How* does one share one's faith?" is legitimate. We cannot simply stop with, Has the faith been shared? but we must go on to ask, Has the faith been shared in a way that does not defeat the selfless nature of the faith? Another way of stating it is to ask, Who has profited most, and in what way, from this exchange, the sharer or the sharee?

What the Bible Says About Motivation

The Bible adds to this problem by presenting seemingly conflicting motivations for preaching the Gospel. On the one hand, there is a strong biblical tradition for "sharing" the Gospel in every sense of the word sharing.

This sharing has many levels: it includes the sharing of the teachings of Jesus in a loving and concerned manner (Eph. 4:1–16), it includes the sharing of food, medicine, and other material help to the poor and the downtrodden of the world (Matt. 25:31–46), and it includes sharing of ourselves in a self-sacrificial way (2 Tim. 2:1–5). The emphasis in these passages and teachings is on the needs of those less fortunate than ourselves. Absent from these lessons is any sense of superiority or triumphalism.

On the other hand, there is an equally strong biblical tradition that what we are doing when we tell others the good news about Jesus Christ is competing for the hearts and minds of humankind.

This competition has many levels: it includes spiritual warfare with the principalities and powers in this world that threaten the very existence of the church (Eph. 6:10–18; Col. 2;15), it includes a command for each of us to be personally ready to answer any and all questions about our faith (1 Peter 3:15), and it includes standing fast even when the going gets tough (Acts 5:17–32; Eph. 6:13–18). The emphasis in these passages is on witnessing to the truth and rightness of the Christian faith and protecting the integrity of that faith in the face of competing ideologies.

We not only have a variety of methods at our disposal for telling others the Good News of Jesus Christ; we also have a spectrum of motivations which fuel our desire to do it, ranging from mutual sharing to out-and-out competition. How do we sort out the methods and motivations that are right for us?

The great communicator of the early church was the apostle Paul, and in the letters he wrote to his new churches, he sometimes talked about his missionary strategy. One particular comment will help us begin to fashion an answer to our question in this chapter. In his first letter to the church at Corinth, Paul makes this comment: "Though I am free and belong to no man, I make myself a slave to everyone, to win as many as possible. . . . I have become all things to all men so that by all possible means I might save some" (9:19–22).

When Paul says he became all things to all people, he is not saying that anything goes in the sharing of the Gospel. At other places he makes it very clear that the message is sacrosanct, that there are some things the missionary cannot do, and that there are some people who will not hear no matter what you do. Paul is not suggesting pragmatism as the standard for measuring missionary effectiveness.

Paul is suggesting, however, that we take both the motivation of the sharer and the motivation of the person being shared with into consideration as legitimate and necessary parts of communicating the Gospel. "To the Jews I became like a Jew" (v. 20), he said, and "to the weak I became weak" (v. 22). We need to examine our own motivations for sharing the Gospel, and we need to consider where the other person is coming from. That knowledge might determine how we share the Gospel story and what form we put it in.

The Share/Compete Spectrum

Since this may sound complicated, I will try to diagram it. Consider it in the form of two complementary spectrums: on one spectrum is the attitude of the person telling the Gospel story. That person may be driven largely by a sharing mentality. She or he is a warm, loving people person who enjoys telling her or his faith journey to others in a one-on-one setting. Or that person may more naturally fall into the category of those who gravitate toward the competitive end of the spectrum. She or he prefer to champion a theological system or preach the Gospel in a public forum.

Of course, the two ends of the spectrum are not mutually exclusive. A person may fall at either end of the spectrum, depending on the time or setting. Although most people probably have a "default" style of witnessing, one they usually feel most comfortable with, some are good at more than one method and feel comfortable in a variety of styles.

We are not talking about right and wrong styles but simply about different styles that people adopt for a variety of reasons. All are good if they follow the New Testament teachings and models, and God uses all to accomplish his purposes.

The second spectrum is that of the people to whom we are telling the Gospel story. We sometimes forget that they have their own religious beliefs, and they may be trying to tell us their story (the dhamma story, or Veda story, or Quran story) even as we are trying to tell them ours. In telling us their story, they use different styles too, and bring different attitudes to the exchange. Let us plot their styles along a spectrum similar to the one we have constructed from the biblical materials: it ranges from a sharing style to a competing style and includes all points in between.

Putting the two spectrums together, we get a diagram that looks like this:

The Christian's Attitude

The Non-Christian's Attitude	*Share*	*Compete*
Share	Share/Share	Share/Compete
Compete	Compete/Share	Compete/Compete

What the apostle Paul was saying to the Corinthians when he said that he was willing to become all things to all people for the sake of the Gospel, is that he was willing to consider where non-Christians were on the share/compete spectrum and adjust his own methodology accordingly. As you can see from the diagram, these possibilities can be divided into four main categories. Each of these categories, because of the nature of the people involved, has methods that naturally fall into it. Each has paradigm biblical examples, and each has specific dangers to which an overemphasis on one aspect or another can lead.

The Four Categories

1. Share/Share. In America's neighborhoods, the share/share quadrant might be the most common. This is the kind of spiritual talk that takes place over a cup of coffee or in backyard lawn chairs between people who have achieved varying degrees of relationship, from growing acquaintance to good friends.

People involved in this kind of sharing most often are those who, because of upbringing, cultural expectations, or temperament, feel comfortable talking about their spiritual journey. Because their own journey is so important to them, they tend to learn from the story of other people's quests. Often the learning takes the form of inspiration: hearing how others have overcome difficulties and doubts inspires them to keep on the spiritual track themselves. Sometimes, though, concrete hints about how to persevere in the quest come from these mutual sharings.

In the one-to-one setting, it usually takes two to share. The non-Christian must also be someone who feels comfortable and learns from this kind of personal interaction. Just as not all Christians feel comfortable with this style, not all Buddhists, Muslims, or Christian Scientists feel comfortable with it.

The share/share mode is perhaps best illustrated by

Peter's witness to the Roman centurion Cornelius in Acts 10. Interestingly, the contact is initiated by Cornelius; he invites Peter to come and tell him about his beliefs. When Peter comes, Cornelius is quite prepared to treat Peter as a religious authority. Peter, however, goes out of his way to put the contact on a person-to-person, conversation-between-equals level. "I am only a man myself" (v. 26), he says in response to Cornelius's adulation. And he dismisses Jewish regulation against visiting non-Jews by saying, "God has shown me that I should not call any man impure or unclean" (v. 28). Then, instead of directing the encounter, he asks Cornelius what the agenda is for their conversation.

This example of the share/share mode is well supported by a number of New Testament teachings advocating love for all people (fellow believers, neighbors, enemies), the danger of a judgmental attitude toward others (especially Matt. 7:1–5), a definite sense of humility about oneself (1 Cor. 2:1–5; Phil. 2:1–11), and a willingness to help others in need, just as the Good Samaritan did, even when a verbal exchange of the Gospel is not part of the encounter. The sharing mode is well attested in Scripture.

Note the elements necessary for this kind of conversation: two people willing to talk in a personal way about faith, a certain level of knowledge (or at least interest) in the other person's religion, and a nonjudgmental attitude toward the other person, even as the conversation might turn toward a gentle comparison of the beliefs.

The danger of this kind of religious interaction is that one of its main strengths, the focus on religious feelings, will so dominate the conversation that the necessity of choice, common and essential to all religions, will be muted or lost. The danger is that we become so caught up in the magic that happens when two human beings talk on the deepest of levels that the essential differences between what we believe will be obscured.

The magic of human relationship will carry us only so far. Sooner or later we discover that the relationship itself must be grounded in something deeper and more substantial than simple feeling. The danger of share/share interaction is that the concept of truth may be obscured. That is not a judgment on share/share interaction. In proper context, it is a wonderful way to communicate the Gospel and to grow in our own faith. Even those who do not feel comfortable with this kind of exchange should force themselves to do it sometimes, simply because there is an element of faith that cannot be communicated in any other way.

2. *Share/Compete.* Sometimes we get in situations where we, because of our style, the possibilities of the situation, or the leading of the Spirit, feel compelled to adopt the share mode, but we find ourselves sharing with people who have no inclination toward adopting the share mode themselves. They are definitely heavy on the compete end of things.

Perhaps the strongest example of this I have come across was on a trip to Egypt I took several years ago. Modern Egypt is a Muslim country, and Christians are forbidden to evangelize there. Needless to say, this puts a real crimp in traditional mission strategy. What was I to do?

What is left to Christians who cannot compete openly or find partners for mutual sharing is to share in a form that will relate even to those who adopt an extreme competing posture. In Egypt I found this took the form of medical help for the sick, economic help for the poor, and birth-control programs for those with already large families. Each of these programs addressed a significant need. They were shared with no hope of material return, a basic tenet of the Gospel story. And they were all programs built on Christian values, values that even though they were not explicitly stated so as to conform with the laws of the land, were by themselves able to carry the freight of the Gospel story to those who wanted to learn it.

This kind of need-oriented sharing has an essential place in our relationship to non-Christians. It recognizes several central truths of the Christian faith: that we are called to help other people no matter what the return or their attitude toward us, that helping in a material way has lasting spiritual value, and that sometimes it is all we can do.

Jesus himself is perhaps the greatest example and promoter of the share/compete mode. Finding himself in a hostile environment, he was often reduced to telling cryptic stories that only those who "had ears to hear" would understand (e.g., Mark 4:9–12; 8:17–23). Under hostile questioning he sometimes remained silent (Mark 15:5). Yet doing something under such circumstances is required, and Jesus made it clear that helping the needy of the world was one of those things (Matt. 25:40).

Even when need-oriented ministry is not all we can do, it is sometimes a more accurate representation of the Gospel than anything else. What is often called lifestyle witnessing is the domestic version of the share/compete mode. It recognizes the essential unity of human beings: that as created creatures we are material as well as spiritual, that the material side of creation is good (although damaged by the Fall), and that it needs to be supported in a God-recognizing way. A Gospel reduced to words alone implies that the mental/spiritual side of our humanity is more real and important than the material.

The danger, of course, is that we might find ourselves thinking that feeding the hungry, healing the sick, and housing the homeless is all there is to the Gospel. This becomes especially tempting in a world where abstract Christian theology has become so confusing and contentious that truth seems beyond us all. It is much simpler, we are tempted to think, to do what we can to raise money, provide for physical needs, and leave the rest for God to settle.

Tempting as this is, it is incomplete. It sidesteps the responsibility to show how the story of Jesus Christ relates to a very differentiated, confusing world. Sharing wealth is important, but it cannot be seen as the only thing we have to share.

3. Compete/Share. As we noted earlier, the Scriptures teach that there is a sense of legitimate competition in presenting the Gospel. We do have a truth to tell, and truth can only be fully articulated when it is set over against what it is not. In and of themselves Christians are no better than non-Christians, but Christian truth is the final form of the truth given to us by God.

The compete/share model is perhaps the one that has most characterized the history of Christian mission. The form most accommodating to it is preaching. The preacher has a set piece to say, and the audience listens and either accepts or rejects what the preacher has to say. Because the audience's role is passive, the people most often attracted to be part of an audience, and surely the ones who most often respond in such a setting, tend themselves to be from the sharing end of the spectrum. They come predisposed to listen. They come already looking for something and usually hoping that they will at last find it here.

The one who competes often knowingly targets the needs of this kind of audience beforehand. Jesus knew who Nicodemus was and what his problem was before he spoke to him. He knew the words he should say about the Gospel that would most appeal to someone in Nicodemus's situation. He said those words and Nicodemus responded. Needless to say, the compete/share model is very effective when done properly.

Unfortunately, it is also an easily abused model. Communicators who tend toward the compete end of the spectrum tend to be powerful people oriented toward measuring success by the ruler of effectiveness. People most attracted to public rallies and sermon settings tend to be open and willing to accept authority. The potential for abuse here is great.

Several years ago a friend told me of his experience preaching to an audience at a Pentecostal rally: "It was heady," he said. "The people were so open to the Spirit, I felt like I could lead them anywhere. At first I thought that was great. Then I got scared. I began to think about what I could do in such a setting."

In that type of situation, manipulation becomes a real temptation. Intentional manipulation is perhaps not the rule, but unintended or well-intentioned manipulation is equally destructive. Thus, this kind of telling of the Gospel demands that the motives of the communicator be constantly checked against some kind of standard.

4. Compete/Compete. This sounds like the most unspiritual of all methods. In some cases it can be. It can degenerate into an unprincipled debate or theological argument easier than any of the other combinations. The competitive nature of both parties can accelerate the conversation to argument status and sometimes beyond that to open hostility.

It need not, however, sink into hostility. Reasoned argument is an important part of the faith, and every religious tradition needs good apologists for its belief system. Christianity is no exception. The key is to keep theological discussion from getting out of hand. Since Christian competitors can do nothing about their non-Christian counterpart's competitive balance, all they can do is make sure that they keep their side of the discussion on an even keel.

One of the greatest opportunities for this kind of competitive exchange is in Utah, where the Church of Jesus Christ of Latter Day Saints is the dominant religion. Churches in this part of the country find themselves constantly challenged to show how the Gospel they preach differs from that taught in Mormon temples. This is made particularly difficult because Mormons use much of the same terminology as Christians do and claim much of Christian history. Furthermore, initially the meanings seem the same. It is only when put in the larger context of the entire religious system that the differences become apparent.

For example, Mormons believe in the Trinity. That belief, however, means they believe in a plurality of gods, that God the Father, God the Son, and God the Holy Spirit, are all three individual gods in their own right, with a common purpose, but distinct beings. Also, they believe there are many God the Fathers and that ultimately, our spiritual goal is to become one of those Gods, with our own human families.

Obviously, a careful understanding of Mormon theology and Mormon use of Christian terms is essential to maintain important distinctions. Compete/compete relationships can help this happen.

Even with the best of intentions, compete/compete contacts can get out of hand. In these situations, Jesus suggested a course of action to take. When Jesus sent the apostles out two by two to preach, he suggested that there would be some occasions that they would have to simply shake the dust off their sandals and move on. The apostle Paul was an expert in compete/compete settings. He debated in synagogues and marketplaces, firmly committed to Christian truth but always open to respectful listening. Sometimes these "conversations" created anger and separation (e.g., Acts 13:13-51). When the competition becomes unfair or refuses to listen, separation may be the only option. But fighting fire with fire is not an option if fighting means sinking to using the manipulative methods of non-Christian,.

On the other hand, there is no better way to sharpen our own doctrines and creeds than to see how they stack up against well-articulated non-Christian doctrines. It is in these settings that we find the weaknesses in our expressions of faith. It is here that we learn forgotten truth that other religions have kept alive. It is here that we learn how to express our creed most effectively. Thus, we need to work very hard to made sure that compete/compete opportunities are a regular part of the body of Christ's agenda in every religious and cultural setting.

The chief danger of sharing in a different cultural setting is that in our efforts to make the Christian message appealing or convincing, we unknowingly change the essence of the message. The way to avoid this is never to engage in such interaction without preparation and without wise Christian partners.

Preach the Truth in Love

Sharing the faith with our non-Christian neighbors can mean various things, and all of them, if done within the parameters of good Christian practice, are appropriate. As we have seen, however, recognizing and labeling our methods and our motives for those methods, and doing the same for our non-Christian neighbors, gives us tremendous advantages in effective sharing and in loving our neighbors according to Christ's command. At times this will mean changing our methods and recognizing changes in their methods. It may mean giving up some method or story in certain situations, but in the long run, the result will be worth the care we take to preach the truth in love.

11

What Should I Do If They Don't Respond?

STATISTICS TELL US THAT NO MATTER HOW YOU tell non-Christians about the Gospel, many will not respond by accepting Jesus Christ as Savior. What do you do then? Interestingly, the options are pretty much the same no matter what answer you gave to the questions of the two preceding chapters. No matter what you think about the question of who is saved and who is not, and no matter what method you use to obey God's command to communicate the Gospel story to others, the basic options if they reject you are similar.

What are the basic options? Two: love them or leave them. You can continue to have some kind of relationship with these non-Christian neighbors, or you can break off contact. Let us look at those options in turn, starting with the "leave them" option.

Leave Them

For many, the leave them option seems the most logical. We are here in the midst of a spiritual war, the argument goes, and we have lost a battle to the enemy. The thing to do is to cut our losses, withdraw, regroup, and get ready to fight again another day.

One Scripture passage often cited to support this option is

Luke 9:5, which records Jesus sending out the twelve disciples to preach the kingdom of God and to heal the sick. He told them that wherever they were not received, they were to shake the dust from their feet as a testimony against them.

In understanding this recommendation we must remember that to not offer someone basic hospitality in first-century Palestine (which it appears is what "whoever will not receive you" means) was an act of more than just bad manners. It was hostile. The basic cultural pattern was to offer a weary traveler water with which to wash, food to eat, and a place to sleep. This was incumbent on the residents whether they agreed with the politics and religion of the travelers or not.

The sandal-shaking ceremony here was not aimed at people who had simply rejected the message of the kingdom of God, although that may have been a part of the rejection. It was aimed at people who had denied the disciples the common courtesies of the day. As we saw in the last chapter, it was for people who had taken the legitimate competition motif and turned it into a hostile attitude that left no room for discussion. Far from being an appropriate passage for arguing the "leave them" option, it could probably more accurately be used as an argument for us to love non-Christians even though they reject the message we bring. The basic courtesies of life are still a part of the Christian witness.

Probably a stronger argument for the "leave them" option can be mounted from a look at the history of Christianity and religion in general. Over the years keeping the faith pure (whatever faith it is we are talking about) has required some pretty strong actions to be taken against people who reject that faith. Some of these actions, upon reflection, seem extreme, but all have been features of both the spread of Christianity and of other religions.

The holy war rationale. Both the history of Christianity and of Islam have startling testimony to the option of trying to force reluctant non-Christians (or non-Muslims) to embrace the faith at the point of the sword. When considered in context, throughout the histories of these two religions the actual number of cases of forced conversion are few. Nevertheless, there are some. Arguments promoting this option range from scriptural (especially Old Testament) models to the tough love argument: We are doing what is best for these people, whether they know it or not.

Today most American Christians look at the holy war option with justifiable distaste. Individual religious freedom has become an inalienable right, protected by both law and public sentiment. However, there is still an attitude toward non-Christians that reflects holy war thinking. *So, they think they are too good to become Christians,* the attitude goes. *Well, okay for them.*

The "okay for them" part means that we will cut them off from mainstream neighborhood society. We will not invite them to our homes, we will not elect them to the PTA board, we will not consider their views when neighborhood action is required. In short, we will ostracize them from having a representative presence in our society.

This may not seem like holy war thinking, but the effect of punishing non-Christians for not seeing the light of the Gospel has basically the same dynamics. It is the "leave them" option with a physical and psychological kicker.

The birds of a feather rationale. Many who reject any form of holy war thinking, whether physical, cultural, or psychological, may be more attracted to the birds of a feather rationale. This means that we simply avoid those who have rejected the Christian message because we have so little in common with them.

In many ways, this is the path of least resistance. The way we think about religious questions does influence our lives in more ways than we think. Thus, our religious beliefs, to some extent at least, heavily influence the way we spend our leisure and family time and the way we spend Sunday. We naturally spend more time with those who think like we do than we do with people whose religious ideas lead them in different directions. Since we are going in different directions, we naturally spend less time together. It is a short step from simply letting these inclinations take their course to avoiding non-Christians altogether.

The values protection rationale. Some choose this reasoning because of a certain way of looking at other religions in the first place. It might be called the disease approach to non-Christian religions. We see other religions as diseases. In attempting to cure these diseases (by evangelism), we must come into limited contact with the carriers of the diseases (our neighbors). We always wash ourselves thoroughly after contact, and when it becomes evident that the disease is fatal and hopeless, we cease contact altogether, sometimes through a slow process of withdrawal, sometimes more abruptly.

The fear, of course, is that either we or our children will catch the disease. This usually is couched not in germ terms, but in values terms. We want our neighborhood to reflect good, solid Christian values, not the values of other religions.

Although I have tried to present these three rationales as being valid for Christians, it surely must be obvious that I do not think they are true to the Christian ideal. I suppose most readers would agree with me on the holy war rationale. The ethos of individual freedom so prevalent in our country would insure that resistance, whether you are a conservative Christian or not.

But I also reject the other two lines of thinking. I reject the birds of a feather rationale because it is not true to the model Jesus gave us for associating with people quite unlike ourselves, such as "tax collectors and sinners" (Mark 2:15–17). By his actions, Jesus taught us to be a witness to God's grace no matter what the social setting. I reject the values protection rationale because, as I have already said elsewhere, there is a core of values common to all religions that we can join together to endorse, even though we may disagree on the source of those values or on where they are leading us. The presence of non-Christian religions does not threaten our values anywhere near as much as the secularist materialism so common to Americans does.

If there is a "threat," it is better seen in the context of the church as an institution. The church does represent the Gospel of the body of Christ to the world. This means that sometimes the church must separate itself from alliances that might give the impression of endorsing non-Christian beliefs. Keeping the faith pure is something the church must be concerned with, but even then we are usually more conservative than we need to be. On an individual level, we are almost always more conservative in our contact than we need to be. Again, we often resist based on psychological factors (shyness, self-centeredness), rather than on theological factors.

But I reject the "leave them" position most of all because it is not consistent with a positive teaching of the Gospel, a teaching that forms the core argument for the "love them" position.

Love Them

We have already discussed how the commands in the Old and New Testaments to love your neighbor are unconditional. It does not make any difference who the neighbors are or what they believe, we are to love them with all of God's love we can muster. Ideally, the fact that they have rejected our well-intentioned presentation of the Gospel should not change that.

But two problems seem to be at work here. The first is that there is a natural reluctance to stay close to someone who has in effect rejected that which is most important to us. For most of us, our religious beliefs are central to our lives. When people reject them, we experience hurt. No matter how sensitively others decide to decline our way of life, we still feel rejected personally. It takes some real effort to overcome the distance that develops and go on from there.

This first problem is a problem of human nature. Like all

such problems, it must be overcome with a will to fulfill God's command to love neighbors, including non-Christian ones. Just as friends who have had an argument eventually bury the hatchet and make up, so we can, with time perhaps, learn to reestablish our relationship with our non-Christian neighbors.

The second problem is more of a philosophical one. It takes the form of a rationalization on why we should in some cases hold in abeyance God's command to love our neighbors, especially the non-Christian ones. In some cases, the rationalization goes, we are justified in not acting on our love for neighbors who have rejected the kingdom of God, because to do so would imply that we think the position they have taken is all right. Continuing to "love" them would be unfair to them, because it would send the wrong signals about what we think the truth is. Therefore, we must communicate our displeasure by withholding our "love."

In a sense, this position rightly views the love of God which we mediate to others through our lives to be a very powerful and valuable force. It is not something we should take lightly, nor is it something we should cast about profligately without making sure its value is known. This position, however, wrongly views the love of God as something we should hold in reserve, a treat to be dispensed as a reward for right actions on the part of others.

As a college student I worked in the psychology lab training pigeons to peck at certain disks in their cages and to ignore others. We would reward them for the right pecks with kernels of corn. To get them to begin pecking in the first place, we would "shape" their behavior by rewarding successively correct moves toward the pecking behavior desired: first, just moving toward the disk, then looking at the disk, and finally only pecking the right disk would bring the reward.

Some, unconsciously perhaps, view Christian love and fellowship in the same way. We reward others with our friendship and concern only if we see them slowly moving toward adopting Christian beliefs and lifestyles. We "shape" their behavior as it more and more matches our ideal. If they give up smoking, we reward them with a dinner invitation; if they quit sharing their faith, we go to a ball game together. If they "backslide" by installing a Buddha image in their backyard, we "punish" them by refusing to have an iced tea gathering on their patio.

This view of Christian love as a behavioral shaping force falls short of the Christian ideal on several counts. First and foremost, it ascribes to ourselves a role in controlling this ultimate power of love that we simply do not possess. The Bible tells us that God dispenses his love on the just and unjust alike. We are simply middlemen and middlewomen in the exchange; God's grace is available to all in unlimited quantities. We are witnesses to the power of this love, but we do not control it at all.

Second, even if we thought we could control behavior in some way by this means, are we so sure we know what kind of behavior to shape in someone else? We may be right on some of the broad strokes, but doesn't everyone find his or her own way with God as guide? Only God knows what he wants the life of our neighbor to become. We can look for signs of God's grace in that person's life and affirm that grace (if we must use behavioral psychological terms!), but we are not up to the task of determining what those signs should be.

Loving our neighbors is unconditional. We really have no options when it comes to our general response to those to whom we have unsuccessfully presented the Gospel. We must continue to love them. A more fruitful question might be *How?*

The Signs of Love

Continue to be Christian witnesses. Just as we have no choice about whether to continue to love our neighbors, we also have no choice about whether to continue to witness to them. Part of our love is our witness, and part of our witness is our love.

"But they have rejected our witness," I can hear you say. "What more can we do?" The answer is that the New Testament models a tremendous variety in how to witness. Much of our witness to others is simply how we live our lives and carry out the everyday business of being good neighbors. Do not think that such seemingly insignificant things go unnoticed.

Do not bug them. Still, we must recognize that something about the way in which we presented the Gospel was ineffective. It turned our neighbors off. Perhaps we presented an image that raised up bad associations from their childhood. Perhaps something jarred them personally. Perhaps the style we used was culturally offensive to them.

Of course, we know that the core story of the Gospel, the claim that sin is a universal trait of all people and that Jesus came to die on the cross for our sins, can be an offense to the way some people think. We dare not mute that truth, even at the risk of offense. But there is a danger that we will continue to offend in some seemingly insignificant way, and our neighbors will mistakenly associate that offense with the essence of the Gospel. Mahatma Gandhi, in his autobiography, *The Story of My Experiments with Truth*, tells of his experiences with Christianity as a young man:

> Christian missionaries used to stand in a corner near the high school and hold forth, pouring abuse on Hindus and their gods. I could not endure this. I must have stood there to hear them once only, but that was enough to dissuade me from repeating the experiment. About the same time, I heard of a well known Hindu having been converted to Christianity. It was the talk of the town that, when he was baptized, he had to eat beef and drink liquor, that he also had to change his clothes, and that thenceforth he began to go about in European costume including a hat. These things got on my nerves. Surely, thought I, a religion that compelled one to eat beef, drink liquor, and change one's own clothes did not deserve the name.[1]

People of some cultures, even cultures transplanted to the United States from other parts of the world, are very sensitive about talking religion until they get to know people very well. Others are offended if you do not talk about religion. For some the timing and place are all important. Talking about Jesus Christ at one time and place may be entirely acceptable and appropriate, but at another time be totally out of place. Sensitizing ourselves to these differences can make all the difference in the world.

Respect their beliefs. The one thing that perhaps offends more than any other is a needless belittling of another person's religion. Usually we do this unintentionally. In our zeal to tell about what is most important to us, we sometimes are too quick to rush to a comparison of our beliefs with religious systems that do not quite measure up from our point of view. Whenever we get the urge to do this kind of comparison, we should ask ourselves two questions: How offensive will this be? and, Is it really necessary to make my point?

In the first place, we probably underestimate how offensive this belittling is. The easiest way to assess this is to think about how we feel when we see our own religion hostilely judged—when Madelyn Murray O'Hair says that God does not exist, when the American Civil Liberties Union files suit against those who publicly display nativity scenes, when humanists question the integrity of Jesus Christ, when the Supreme Court says that prayer in public places is unconstitutional. Our initial reaction to such judgments is usually anger.

In a similar way, even the most innocent comments and questions about other people's religious beliefs run the danger of needless offense. As in the case of Gandhi, who saw a whole culture and way of life judged by the comments and actions of a few, we need to be careful how we approach our neighbors and their way of life.

In the second place, we probably do not realize how unnecessary it is to say negative things about another's religion. The story of what God did through Jesus Christ has enough power to stand on its own. It does not need the belittling of other stories to carry the freight of the Gospel meaning. We can feel comfortable that the power inherent in the Gospel story will do its own convicting, even without whatever editorial emendations we add to it. So why should we jeopardize the power of this story by needlessly judging other people's religions? After the power of the Gospel story grabs hold of our neighbors in a way they have never been grabbed before, they will probably begin to make some comparisons themselves, and they may ask questions and solicit our help in such comparisons. But until they are ready for such help and ask for it, it is unwise to present them with comparisons.

At the same time, we can learn a great deal ourselves from what other people tell us about their beliefs. We should not be quick to reject everything they say, for they may give us insights that will remarkably enlighten forgotten facets of our own Christian faith.

What Does Communicate?

There is no definitive answer to this question. Rather, there are different answers in different situations. I remember one story of real Gospel communication, however, that impresses me as one that would work well in any neighborhood setting. Two neighbors were as different as night and day in the way they looked at life. One was a lifelong Democrat, the other a Republican. One had been a successful businessman for many years, while the other worked for a succession of public watchdog organizations, the latest an environmental group. One was a solid Christian, the other did not even darken the door of the church on Christmas and Easter.

But for some reason they got along. They did not talk business or politics or religion much—that was a surefire formula for an argument. But they did talk life over the back fence often: their yard work, their kids and school, their marriages. When the non-Christian's wife was diagnosed with a particularly virulent form of cancer and went from total health to death in three months, it was the neighbor who stepped in the breach.

The husband recalled the night of his wife's death: "I was in total despair. I went through the funeral preparations and the service like I was in a trance. And that night after the service, I just wanted to be alone. I left and went to the path along the river in our town and walked all night. But I did not walk alone. My neighbor, afraid for me, I suppose, stayed with me all night. He did not speak; he did not try and get me to go home; he did not even walk beside me. He just followed me. When the sun finally came up over the river the next morning, he came up to me and said, 'Let's get some breakfast.'

"I go to church now, my neighbor's church. I do not really like the pastor's politics sometimes. But a religion that can produce the kind of caring and love my neighbor showed me is something I want to be involved in. I want to be like that. I want to love and be loved like that the rest of my life."

12

Being a Good Neighbor to Non-Christians

WE LIVE IN A UNIQUE TIME, A TIME OF UNPARALLELED religious freedom and diversity. The uniqueness lies not only in the scores of religions, ethnic groups, and nationalities that live among us; it lies especially in the fact that for the first time in history we have a society that protects and endorses religious diversity economically, legally, politically, and, in most cases, culturally. People of all religions enjoy full protection in our courts; they make the same amounts of money; they vote, run for office, and lobby in equal measure; and our culture—the arts, education, leisure groups, and media—for the most part supports the diversity of religions.

You will note that twice I qualified our cultural support for the diversity of religions. The hedging comes when I consider two important parts of our culture that have not fully come to grips with it: families and churches. American families and churches have ambiguous feelings about their new religious neighbors. When it comes to private life, the right for each of us to worship God, the gods, or the transcendent, our families and churches almost always lend full support to this freedom. But when it comes to public life, we still struggle with the concept. What does religious freedom mean when we apply it to both private and public life, when we concede that the United States is not a Christian nation but a nation that supports Christians—along with Hindus, Buddhists, Jews, Muslims, Mormons, Moonies, New Agers, and, yes, secularists?

A pastor in Aurora, Illinois articulated this struggle very well during a controversy in his town over the building of a Hindu temple two blocks from his church. "I believe in the right of these people to worship as they please," he said. "I know if I do not give them this freedom, then my own religious freedom is in jeopardy. But I'm frankly worried about what this means for my children. I do not want them to be influenced by non-Christian values in our schools and neighborhoods." He paused for a moment and then, looking at me, smiled and said, "That sounds confusing, doesn't it?"

As we have looked in this book at some of the more difficult questions facing us in this age of religious pluralism, that one word—*confusion*—typifies more readers' thoughts and feelings about the issue than any other. We are torn between two equally strong forces that seem irreconcilable in this climate: (1) our strong belief in religious freedom for all, and (2) our full commitment to furthering the cause of the Christian church. How can we be both tolerant and committed? How can we love our neighbor and preach the truth?

In this final chapter, I would like to pull together in succinct, preliminary form some of the possible implications of the situations I describe throughout this book. I have argued in chapter after chapter that we can both support religious freedom and still be fully engaged in the cause of Christ. To do so, we need to uncover the secret key that makes this difficult task possible; we need to fully understand what is at stake if we do not step up to this challenge; and we need to look at the three main tasks that confront us in the immediate future in order to make carrying out this challenge possible.

The Secret Key

I will start by defining (defending?) my rather melodramatic heading: secret key. I call it a *key* because I think the dynamic I am going to describe is the essential one in order for a democratic, religiously plural climate with a Christian majority to function. I call it *secret*, because I think that up to this point it has been functioning, albeit anonymously. Without it, we would have seen public movements to endorse the majority religion (Christianity), wholesale persecution of people of non-Christian religions, or riots in the streets. We have not seen any of these three movements, largely, I think, because of the secret key. This key needs to be articulated, made public, and refined so that it can be consciously endorsed by all. Is it too melodramatic to say that if we do not, one of the three things I just mentioned might happen in the future?

The key is a common value system. We have a common value system in the United States, and we are coming closer and closer to having one worldwide. I am not telling any secrets here. It has been convincingly shown by a number of writers, theologians, and historians of religion that a *tao* (as C. S. Lewis called it) exists. This common moral code argues that human beings should not kill one another, lie to one another, steal from one another, or cheat in relationships sexual and otherwise, and that they should work together for the common good. All of the major world religions teach these things. Religions that do not teach them either die out or exist as antireligions, recognized by all as such and surviving only because they feed off the energy of the mainstream religion and culture.

Some Christian theologians object to the notion of a common moral code, and they use two arguments to do so. The first argument is that a common moral code must be based on the existence of some natural law common to all people and discoverable by human effort and reasoning. Since this natural law, to be valid, must remain outside the unique revelation of God in Jesus Christ, they argue, it cannot be considered determinative for Christians who base their religion on the uniqueness of Jesus Christ.

Some would want to argue with these theologians on the

basis of the validity of natural law. This is an important and arguable point. It is a debate we have had and need to continue having.

However, that debate is not strictly necessary to show that a common moral code exists for all the religions. We are not speaking about religious truth at this point but about religious "politics." We are looking for something on which to base everyday cooperation. We are saying such a resource exists: one simply has to look at the ethical systems of all the religions—most of which are accepted according to a dynamic very similar to our concept of revelation—and see the common features. For the purposes for which we are identifying this common moral code (living in harmony with religions with which we do not agree), we need not agree on the base of this set of values other than that it exists, and for us it exists because it was revealed to us by God. The concept of natural revelation need not play a determinative part, at least at this stage and for this purpose.

The purpose of the common moral code at this stage is simply to be able to say to one another, *Look, we all agree that these are the elements of the moral code by which we want to live. I know you derive these principles from a different source than I do, but we can at least agree on how we should live. So let's do it.*

The second objection has to do with the look we have just taken at the ethical systems to come up with the elements of the common moral code. That look, some theologians have argued, turns up ethical points on which the religions disagree. Because of these obvious disagreements, they argue, we cannot say that a common moral code exists.

It is true that there are elements of the ethical systems of the different religions that do not agree. Some features (for example, of sexual ethics) are at odds with the different religions. Those disagreements in themselves, however, do not vitiate the broad areas of major agreement. They need not force us to deny that a core exists that we do agree on. That would be like saying that because not all trees are pine trees, pine trees are not the same. They are the same, just as the religions' prohibitions against killing, lying, stealing, unfaithfulness, and injustice are the same.

The common moral code not only exists, it is what has held us together in this country up until now. It has functioned in "secret" for two reasons, one political, the other theological. Politically it has been far safer for lawmakers to ascribe the common moral code to secular law codes or to a secular ideal of natural law (on the rare occasions that ascription has been necessary) than to the religions of the world. Our constitution guarantees separation of church and state, and this has made it unwise for legislators, judges, and others to indiscriminately claim religious roots for their ideals (although many do it to the religious sectors of their constituencies all the time). This has helped us to maintain the admirable goal of separation but has conversely pushed religion to the edges of public life and made future religious conflict almost inevitable.

Theological resistance to identifying the common moral code has come from those who fear that identifying a common moral core might lead to a lessening of Christianity's uniqueness. This is an understandable fear. Many of the most outspoken champions of identifying a common moral code are people in favor of a movement toward one world religion. They have identified the common moral code, not as a mechanism to allow us to live together in peace despite our radical differences, but as part of an attempt to minimize the differences. People of all religions have rightly resisted this movement for reasons we have discussed in previous chapters, but the net result has been to make the idea of a common moral code unpopular.

We need to make this idea fashionable. We need to publicly articulate the common moral code, seek interfaith agreement on it, and recognize that we can use this as our public religious glue (as we already in effect are), even as we firmly commit ourselves to our particularity and uniqueness. Recognition of this common moral code does not mean that we consider all religions to be the same, nor does it mean that we should cease to believe and articulate our understanding of its basis in God's revelation. To the contrary, it is part of our assurance that sometime in the future we will not be forced to all become the same.

What Is at Stake

What is at stake is nothing less than the credibility of Christianity as a life-changing, problem-solving force in the modern world. Can Christianity deal with religious pluralism? Does Christianity have answers that can be applied to this particular political situation? Or is it a religion that can only work when it is aligned with political power or when another religion is in political power and Christianity is persecuted? We know from history that it can work in both of those situations. Can it work in a democratic situation of religious pluralism? Some, including myself, think that it will work best in that situation. Others, apparently, are not so sure.

Over the two-thousand-year history of Christianity we have paid lip service to the concept of Christianity as the conscience of king and peasant alike—of being neither progovernment nor antigovernment. Jesus Christ refused political power, both when Satan offered it to him and when the people egged him on toward it. He chose the notion of being in the world but not of it.

We now—some say for the first time in our history—have the chance to put the "in the world, but not of it" concept to its truest test ever. Will we step up to the challenge or stub our ecclesiastical toes? The temptation to stub our toes is a strong one.

We are tempted by political power. Jesus's rejection of such power during his temptation in the desert forewarns us of the dangers there (Matt. 4:1–11). We are tempted and too often fall. When we fall we find our churches, pastors, and lay leaders manipulated by political parties for unholy ends, entangled in support for the very antithesis of Jesus' message:

wars and rumors of wars, sin and sinners, principalities and powers.

We are tempted by religious power. We preach a religion of love but fight so badly among ourselves that the world surely must wonder where all the love has gone. First Corinthians 13 should be put at the forefront of conflict resolution. Instead, too often we find ourselves leaders of the wolf pack, howling and snapping with glee not only at the heels of the non-Christian religions, but at the heels of fellow Christians who have not toed the line in some "important" way.

The credibility of Christianity is at stake if we do not step up to the challenge of religious pluralism.

What Needs to Be Done

1. Make absolute truth an intellectually respectable position, separate from absolutism.

The most unpopular thing you can do in public life today, whether it be in education, politics, or business is to suggest that there is, somewhere out there a single, absolute standard against which to measure truth.

Do you want to put a real chill on a group conversation at PTA? Say something like, "I believe premarital sex is wrong because the Bible says so."

Here is one that will stop a business lunch dead in its tracks: "There are ethical standards that all the cultures of the world have taught throughout history that we ought to consider in this deal."

The idea that truth is single, absolute, and to some degree knowable is foreign to people's ears these days. When you say anything that closely resembles that belief, people look at you as if you are incredibly naive or an intellectual troglodyte. Of the three things I am suggesting in this chapter, I think the single most important one is this: That we make it intellectually credible to believe in absolute truth. I should be able to say that I am an exclusivist without turning red with the intolerant shame of it all. The relativists among us have done an incredibly effective job of convincing everyone that the religious pluralism of the day demands that the belief that one religion, one philosophy, or one culture might be better than another is subversive.

To be fair, relativism came in response to a new world order that did indeed call into question the old formulations of philosophy and religion. The new things included a new application of science and its resulting technological innovations, a population explosion that has people bumping into each other like never before, and a failure of nerve on the part of the religions of the world to step up to their full responsibilities as the standard-bearers of the spiritual realm. *We must make religion more applicable to this condition of technology and pluralism,* was the cry, and relativism was the answer. The analysis of the itch was correct, but the scratch was off the mark. What might be the correct scratch? I think it needs to be looked for along the following lines:

a. There is a new reality that must be addressed. It is called modernity, and as Robert Bellah has convincingly shown us, it consists in two new elements: unprecedented individual freedom and a plurality of institutional authorities.[1] For religion this means that few people in our culture have much patience with authoritarian pronouncements on religious issues from clergy or church.

b. Relativism has failed dramatically to solve the problem. Institutions that adopt it, whether denomination, political party, education, or business have suffered radical decline. Paradoxically, even though people do not want to be dictated to, they still acknowledge that someone or something inevitably does the dictating.

c. The real solution is to restate the exclusivist position creatively, that is, recognizing that a return to dogmatic institutional authority will not work. We must not sacrifice the gains we have made in individual freedoms, but we must recognize that self-accepted revealed religion necessarily limits our freedom.

At the same time, this renewed commitment to absolute truth must be done even as we disavow absolutism, the attitude that we are the keepers of truth and everyone else is simply wrong or worse. It is this kind of attitude that made it so easy for the relativists to gainsay absolute truth in the first place. We made easy targets. It was not so bad when we claimed absolute truth: philosophically and theologically, the position that absolute truth exists is defensible. What did us in was when we hinted that not only did absolute truth exist, but that we know it absolutely. Not only is this claim arrogant, it is not supported by Scripture. "For now we see in a mirror, dimly" (1 Cor. 13:12, NRSV) is the scriptural wisdom that we too often forget.

To put it simply, there is no reason we cannot at one and the same time defend the concept of absolute truth, and do it with a modest, humble spirit, learning from others as we go. Not only is this logically possible and psychologically healthy, it is theologically orthodox. And our situation of religious pluralism calls for it as never before.

2. Create a forum to talk with the other religions, making common public cause with them when appropriate and necessary.

To understand why this is necessary, we must look briefly at how Christianity and government have related in the United States. For Christians, government exists to protect the general public by maintaining order. In Romans 13 Paul makes clear that even non-Christian rulers, if they maintain good order and do not persecute Christians, are endorsed by God. Part of maintaining good order means keeping the peace between contending political parties, businesses, cultural interests, and, yes, religions. In the political situation of the United States this last task is supposed to be done without endorsing any single religion. All are to be protected; none are to be endorsed. This is called maintaining the separation of church and state.

Historically this has worked well in the United States, largely because almost everyone in the country was Christian. Even though the government did not favor Christianity by name, whenever it did anything to help and protect "religion," it was really helping the religion of the land, Christianity; and because we were all, for practical purposes, Christians, it seemed just fine.

The growth of the non-Christian religions changed that. To live up to the ideal of the separation of church and state, the government had to draw the lines much more sharply. Whenever anything remotely religious was considered—crosses in public buildings, Christmas creches on courthouse lawns, chaplains in the armed forces—government policy had to be scrupulously careful not to favor one religion over the other.

The practical effect of this was that both the government and the courts became more and more distant from any kind of association with religion, even the most common varieties of popular "civil" religion. Civil religion includes things like public prayer, use of the word *God*, and thanksgiving for spiritual blessings. When these things are excised from public display, religion becomes an affair of a person's private life.

This strict separation had the desired effect in terms of fairness to individual religions. Although there is a certain amount of religious intolerance that takes place in the United States, on balance people really can worship as they please here. Compared with situations in the rest of the world, ours is a good system.

However, what was gained in religious fairness has been lost in the role that religion has played in the public affairs of this country. At times religion has been almost totally deleted from our history. Public school textbooks rarely mention it for fear of appearing to favor one religion or another. Ethics—the way people treat one another and the public rules we live by—has always been rooted in religious systems of one sort or another. But in the United States we have for many years now been playing a game of denying that ethics is rooted in religion. The result of this charade has been an extraordinary decline in ethical behavior in business (see recent Wall Street scandals), politics (see the minutes of the United States Senate Ethics Committee meetings for the past five years), and the average person's values (see crime statistics, values surveys, etc.) We have both benefited and suffered from our policy of separation of church and state.

My proposal for a forum of religions in this country is an attempt to maintain the freedom and fairness of our current policy of the separation of church and state, and to address the damage done by the exclusion of religion from public policy-making, indeed, from the public consciousness of Americans in general. To accomplish these two, sometimes conflicting, goals, this forum must have the support of both private religious groups and the government. Neither of these groups can do it alone—nor should they.

The government is restricted because of the constitutional prohibitions against either controlling or favoring specific religions. In many countries, a "Department of Religion" is a standard feature of government, almost always set up to restrictively control religion. In some countries that same department endorses the "one, true religion" to the detriment of the others. But in our country, because of the ideal of separation of church and state, that is impossible.

The religious groups cannot do it alone, either, especially if they want to positively influence the common good of the country. For that, the government connection must somehow be made. Without that connection, the religions will continue to become more and more marginalized, relegated to the private sector of life, having less and less influence on public affairs. Thus, I propose a forum be created that will have representatives of both religious and governmental sectors. This forum would do the following five things:

a. It would serve as a clearinghouse for ideas of religious import that the country needs to hear.

b. It would be a court of conflict resolution, where religious groups can bring complaints to one another regarding persecution, unfair characterization, and misunderstandings, without resorting (at least at first) to courts that cannot, because of the constitutional restrictions, be sensitive to the very nature of religious groups.

c. It would voice to the government religious concerns common to all the religions, especially in the ethical and moral dimensions of legislation.

d. It would offer the government a place to air its concerns to the religious groups of America, regarding things like nonprofit status, fund-raising, religion in education, and church/state issues of various kinds.

e. It would give the religious groups of America a chance to speak to the world on issues of religious freedom, human rights, and political misuse of their brothers and sisters in foreign lands.

Currently some of these purposes are being carried out by a number of different groups. Pluralism is calling us to do some consolidation, perhaps starting with an umbrella group that would pull some of these functions under one roof.

This forum would not do away with either the right or the need for individual religions (and within religions, denominations) to separately voice their own concerns to the American public. The religious institutions currently set up for that purpose would still be needed and important. Individual religious groups would not be bound by their association in this forum to remain silent on issues of individual concern. In fact, the forum would encourage them to make their statements.

3. Live the hope that is within us.

One of the distinguishing features of Christianity is the strong emphasis it gives to the concept of hope. In the context in which Christianity grew up, hope had a quite different meaning. The Greeks and Romans basically viewed hope as neither good nor bad. Hope meant that one could expect either good or evil to come, but this expectation did not carry any positive meaning. In fact, some of the Greek philosophers treated hope cynically, seeing it as a human weakness.

Christianity does not denigrate human hope. In fact, the Bible describes Christ himself as the hope of all humanity. Paul saw himself as an apostle of "Christ Jesus our hope" (1 Tim. 1:1). Of the three essential graces—faith, love, and hope—hope is the one that applies to the future, that ensures us that no matter what has happened in the past and what happens today, the future holds the greatest promise.

We live in a day where a future of great promise seems to many to be a dim hope indeed. The threat of nuclear catastrophe, environmental destruction, and public secularism hang like Damoclean swords over our vulnerable heads, suspended by the flimsiest of threads.

Christ did not deny the sword hanging over our heads. What Christ did do was say that for Christians the thread is not flimsy, but is actually a steel rope, incapable of being broken. For Christians, the dangers of the world are real and are there for all to see and temporarily, at least, experience; but Christ has taken away the threat and replaced it with the promise of eternal life. That is the Christian hope.

How many of us live with that kind of hope? In a world where despair, depression, and loneliness are growing at unprecedented rates, the best witness we can offer our neighbors is to live the hope that is within us; to recognize the dangers, toils, and snares of this world; but by the way we live, talk, and relate, to show the world that God's grace will pull us through. That is the great truth of Christianity. That is the great gift we have to give to a sorrowing, confused, pluralistic world.

Notes

CHAPTER 1

[1]Terry Muck, *Alien Gods on American Turf* (Wheaton: Scripture Press, 1990).

[2]*New York Times* (September 11, 1990).

[3]Muck, *Alien Gods,* 21–31.

[4]*Daily Texan* (October 2, 1990).

CHAPTER 2

[1]See George Gallup, ed., *Religion in America* (Princeton: Princeton Religious Research Center, 1982), 65.

CHAPTER 3

[1]Patrick Buchanan, "Proliferating Islam Knows No Tolerance," *San Antonio Express News* (August 19, 1989), 4-C.

CHAPTER 4

[1]C. S. Lewis, *The Abolition of Man* (New York: Macmillan, 1947), 51–61.

[2]Jeffrey Moses, *Oneness: Great Principles Shared by All Religions* (New York: Fawcett, 1989).

[3]James Patterson and Peter Kimit, *The Day America Told the Truth* (Tappan: Prentice-Hall, 1991).

CHAPTER 7

[1]See the brief note entitled "Interfaith Anxiety" in *Psychology Today* (December, 1988), 6.

CHAPTER 9

[1]Wilfred Cantwell Smith, *The Meaning and End of Religion* (New York: Mentor, 1962).

[2]John Hick, *The Myth of Christian Uniqueness* (Maryknoll, NY: Orbis, 1988), 16–17.

[3]Lesslie Newbigin, *The Gospel in a Pluralistic Society* (Grand Rapids: Eerdmans, 1989), 177–80.

CHAPTER 11

[1]Mahatma Gandhi, *The Story of My Experiments with Truth* (New York: Dover, 1983), 29–30.

CHAPTER 12

[1]Robert Bellah, *Beyond Belief* (New York: Harper & Row, 1970), 20–53.

APPENDIX

[1]Robert McCheyne, as quoted in E. K. Simpson, *Ephesians* (Grand Rapids: Eerdmans, 1957), 100.

Appendix 1
Speaking the Truth in Love

Speaking the Truth

It is fitting that in the passage from which this phrase is taken, Ephesians 4:15, the word used for speaking is a broad one, and most commentators have difficulty deciding whether it actually means spoken words or done deeds. Most, and I will follow them, decide that it means both. It means representing the truth to the world in all we think, say, and do. Thus, it includes preaching, teaching, evangelizing, witnessing, and living as a Christian.

Living as a Christian so that the world can see the truth of the Gospel is not an optional sideline to the Christian life; it is our reason for being. For those tempted to think otherwise—that their Christianity can be a private, non-normative life and that they have the option of sharing their faith publicly—Christ offered strong words. Luke reports Jesus' explanation to his followers of the purpose of his life, death, and resurrection: that "repentance and forgiveness of sins will be preached in his name"; and then he told them what their role would be: "You are witnesses of these things" (Luke 24:47–48). Being a witness is not optional. Christ did not say that we can chose to be witnesses; he said that we *are* witnesses in everything we do.

The mode of witnessing varies. Some are apostles, some prophets, some evangelists, some pastors, some teachers, some caregivers, but all of us are witnesses even as we preach, teach, and love. It is true that in biblical history a particular mode of witnessing may have predominated, according to the needs of the time. In the Old Testament, for example, Noah was a preacher of righteousness, but he "preached" to a sinful age largely by building an apparently useless, landlocked boat miles from any water. Moses witnessed through the giving of the Law—a Law designed to unify and designate God's people as a holy tribe. The prophets risked life and limb by giving unwanted social commentary to kings and other VIPs. John the Baptist retained many of the Old Testament witnessing styles, but added a new one: testifying to an inner kingdom of the spirit that witnessed to the God of Abraham, Isaac, and Jacob as surely as the existence of Israel did. Jesus personified this new kingdom and then sent out apostles to preach to the lost and give instruction to the saved.

No matter what the political situation of the people of God was, no matter who the audience was, and no matter what the skills of individual followers of God were, speaking the truth about God and what he did through his people Israel and his Son Jesus Christ is one constant in all of Scripture. The command to speak the truth about God never varies.

Love Your Neighbor

A second teaching about witnessing also never varies throughout Scripture. This is the teaching about the attitude we must have toward those to whom we witness. We are to love them unconditionally, unreservedly, and without hope of gain. We are to love our neighbors.

The phrase "love your neighbor" first appears in Leviticus 19:18: "Do not seek revenge or bear a grudge against one of your people, but love your neighbor as yourself." Verses in Exodus elaborate on what this means in terms of action: It means, among other things, taking care of even an enemy's oxen or cattle that might wander into one's yard, and it means treating aliens well and giving them hospitality at every opportunity.

So when Jesus taught the concept of loving neighbors, he was not teaching something totally new. Even the radical command of the Sermon on the Mount to love enemies is anticipated by the Old Testament law. Surely Jesus' parable of the Good Samaritan was as unpopular with first-century Palestinians as Equal Opportunity Employment laws are with many twentieth-century Americans, but it was not new.

What was perhaps new was the emphasis Jesus, and Paul after him, gave to this law. Loving neighbors was not one law among many laws; both Jesus and Paul insisted that it was the key law, the central law, the law from which all the other laws were derived. The New Testament book of James demands that loving neighbors as oneself is the "royal law" (Jas. 2:8). Jesus made this emphasis on the Royal Law clear in response to a question put to him by a Pharisee, a Jewish expert in the law, who asked him, "Teacher, which is the greatest commandment in the Law?" " 'Love the Lord your God,' " was Jesus's reply, ". . . and . . . 'Love your neighbor as yourself' " (Matt. 22:36–39).

Both James and Paul emphasized the centrality of the Royal Law by noting that if you fulfilled this one law well, you were forced to fulfill all the other laws by extension. If you love your neighbor as yourself, Paul pointed out, then you would certainly not kill him; neither would you steal from her (would you want to be stolen from?), covet his wife (would you want your spouse to be coveted?), or even lie to him or her. If you truly love your neighbor as yourself, the basis is laid for Gospel-centered living (Rom. 13:8–10; Jas. 2:8–11).

Speaking the truth in love is the appropriate response to adherents of non-Christian religions. An early Christian preacher put it this way: "Truth without love lacks its proper environment and loses its persuasive power; love without truth forfeits its identity, degenerating into maudlin sentiment without solidity, feeling without principle."[1] Together, however, they capture the essence of the Christian Gospel.

Appendix 2
A Neighbor's Guide To Non-Christian Religions

The following is a selective guide to the history, beliefs, and practices of non-Christian religions you are most likely to find in your neighborhood.

Religion	**Approximate Numbers in United States**
Hinduism	2,000,000
Buddhism	2,000,000
Judaism	6,000,000
Islam	4,000,000
Bahai	200,000
Native American	1,500,000
Church of Jesus Christ of Latter-Day Saints	5,000,000
Christian Science	200,000
Unity School of Christianity	3,000,000*
Jehovah's Witnesses	800,000
Unification Church	30,000
New Age	10,000,000*

*users of religous group's services

HINDUISM

Demographics

United States: 2,000,000 (estimated by extrapolating from Indian population). Worldwide: 700,000,000.

Key Dates

2000 B.C. Modern Hinduism is built on an indigenous religion in the Indus Valley, which runs through modern Pakistan and northwest India. The Indus Valley religion emphasized cultic bathing, ritual purity, and cultic interest in fertility.

1500 B.C. A northern European race, sometimes called the Aryans, conquer the Indus Valley peoples and establish Vedism, a religion based on religious writings, called the Vedas, that emphasize ritual and caste.

500 B.C. The Upanishads, religious writings that universalize and interiorize the Vedic rituals, are written.

500 A.D. During this period, the classical doctrines of Hinduism—*brahman, dharma, samsara, karma,* and *moksha*—are established.

1700 A.D. The reformed period of modern Hinduism begins, during which classical Hinduism and modern western and eastern civilizations impact the tradition. This period includes invasions, trading contacts, and Muslim and Christian missionary efforts.

Core Beliefs

Brahman. The universal, all-encompassing principle of truth. The many gods of Hinduism are different manifestations of this single truth.

Dharma. All of existence as we know it operates according to a principle of dharma or law. The key to successful living is becoming tuned in to one's own dharma and then faithfully living it.

Samsara. Reality as we know it. Although our perception of reality is not ultimate reality, we all must live in samsara for many lifetimes.

Karma. The inexorable law of right and wrong. Good deeds bring good fruit (a better life or rebirth) and bad deeds bring bad fruit (a worse life or rebirth).

Moksha. Release or liberation from this worldly life (samsara) into the ultimate monistic state, in which there is neither right nor wrong, positive nor negative. Total identification with Brahman.

Distinctive Practices

Bhakti. Devotion to one of the many gods. In practice, most Hindus identify with one god as their personal god of worship.

Four Goals. The lifestyle all men and women attempt to follow. The goals are material happiness, loving and being loved, doing one's duty, and working to achieve spiritual liberation.

Caste. The four principal castes are priests, leaders, merchants, and servants. A fifth group of people, outcastes, are outside the system with no caste rights whatsoever. In practice, the principal castes are broken down into hundreds of subgroups, called *jati*, focused around occupations.

Four Stages. Student, householder, forest dweller (spiritual seeker), and renouncer. In practice most Hindus do not go beyond householder in this life.

Six Philosophies. Represent different paths or ways of seeking liberation.

Worship Times/Places

Hindu worship is of two main types. *Arati* is the simpler type and involves passing fire or incense in front of a picture or statue of a god. *Puja* is the more elaborate type, in which fruit, flowers, and other ingredients are offered to the deity. Worship takes place both in temples and Hindu homes.

Food

Many Hindus, though not all, are vegetarians. They believe food is of three types: *sattvic* food makes the mind calm (grains, vegetables, fruits); *rajasic* food makes the mind restless (fish, chicken, spices, mild stimulants); and *tamasic* food makes the mind dull (beef, deep-fried foods, hard liquor). Of course, sattvic foods are to be preferred.

Gender, Marriage, Family

In the higher castes, arranged marriages, usually within the caste, are still the rule in India. Often high caste American Hindus send back to India for spouses for their children.

American Versions

Temple Hinduism. Immigrant Hindus often build architecturally exact replicas of Indian Hindu temples. These temples are usually devoted to the worship of a single Hindu deity. *Vishnu, Siva,* and *Shakti* are the most common.

Vedanta Society. A philosophic variety of Hinduism taught by Vivekananda, an early Hindu guru who came to teach in the United States. It has fourteen temples, mainly in large cities.

Hare Krishna. A 1960s version of Hinduism popular with young people who would leave home and family to live in a temple and chant mantras on street corners and in airports. Full name: International Society for Krishna Consciousness; founded by Swami Prabhupada in 1965.

Transcendental Meditation. A popular meditation technique taught by Maharishi Mahesh Yogi. Over 1,000,000 Americans have taken basic TM training.

Gurus. Independent Indian teachers often come to America. Some are orthodox, but some teach highly idiosyncratic versions of Hinduism.

Holidays

Holi. Popular spring festival, celebrated by joyous dancing and feasting.

Dasera. A ten-day festival in autumn, held in honor of goddess Durga (Kali).

Divali. Winter festival associated with New Year and the female goddess Lakshmi and Rama. The theme is prosperity.

Temple Festivals. Usually once each year temples parade their god's image around the village, sometimes changing to a new image (of the same god).

Common Misunderstandings

American Christians have particular difficulty with "idol" worship, often viewing Hindus as indiscriminantly polytheistic. Hindus are polytheistic in a sense, but they see the different gods (estimates of the number are in the hundreds of thousands) as manifestations of the oneness of the universe, Brahman. Thus, they are more properly viewed as pantheistic (god as everything), at least in the philosophical sense.

Current Relationships with Christianity

Most Hindus are friendly toward Christians. In India, early Hindus, when confronted with Christianity, tended to want to absorb it and, in some places, accepted it as a subcaste of Hinduism. Hindus often talk about all religions as pointing to the same underlying reality, Brahman. In practice, most see Hinduism as the the best path to liberation.

Introductory Reading

Scriptures: Many volumes, including Vedas, Upanishads, and the epics. A good anthology is edited by Wendy Doniger O'Flaherty, *Textual Sources for the Study of Hinduism* (Chicago: University of Chicago Press, 1988).

A good basic introduction to Hinduism is R. C. Zaehner, *Hinduism* (New York: Oxford, 1987).

A popular periodical is the monthly newspaper, *Hinduism Today* (Address: 1819 Second Street, Concord, CA 94519; Phone: 510 / 827-0127).

BUDDHISM

Demographics

United States: 3,000,000. Worldwide: 300,000,000.

Key Dates

563–483 B.C. Traditional dates for the life of the Buddha.

483–270 B.C. Following the death of the Buddha, three councils are held; during this period, the Buddha's teachings are debated and standardized among several sects.

270 B.C. to 100 A.D. Asoka is the first ruler of all India to embrace the Buddha's teachings. He encourages their adoption in India and sends missionaries to surrounding countries to spread the word.

100–900 A.D. The age of expansion, during which Buddhism spreads to Sri Lanka in the south; Burma, Thailand, and Vietnam in the east; and China, Japan, and Tibet in the north.

900–1600 A.D. During this period Buddhism adapts itself to the new cultures of Southeast Asia, China, Japan, and Tibet. In each case a distinctive yet recognizably Buddhist form of teaching emerges.

1600 to the present. During the modern age, Buddhism has become a worldwide religion, spreading to Europe and the United States.

Core Beliefs

Buddha. The word literally means "Enlightened One" and describes a person fully aware of the way things really are. Many Buddhas have lived, but Gautama Buddha left us the current teaching.

Dukkha. The word means "suffering." The first truth of the four noble truths of Buddhism teaches that everything about our current existence is suffering. Even the good things that happen to us are temporary (*anicca*).

Paticca-samuppada. The cycle of conditioned existence. Anything that happens is conditioned by something else and occurs in cyclical patterns. The key to enlightenment is to break this endless chain of cause and effect.

Magga. The path that leads to a realization of the truth is called the noble eightfold path: right speech, conduct, and livelihood; right effort, concentration, and meditation; and right views and thoughts.

Anatta. The teaching that even the self is impermanent and there is no ongoing personal entity. Only karmic (good and evil) effects pass from life to life in rebirth.

Nirvana. The final state of enlightenment or emptiness.

Distinctive Practices

Since the goal of Buddhism is individual realization of the truth without the help of gods and goddesses, practices center around the form of personal seeking that each Buddhist takes, that is, meditative practices.

Theravada meditation. Theravada Buddhists rely on three resources: the Buddha as a model of good living, the Buddha's teaching (*dhamma*) as the way to live, and the community of believers (*sangha*) as those who are doing their best to live the life. They practice insight meditation, especially focusing on the breath.

Mahayana meditation. Mahayanists add another resource and ideal to their religious supports, the *bodhisattva.* Bodhisattavas are those beings who achieve enlightenment but who, instead of accepting their final reward, return to help others in their spiritual and meditative practices. There are many bodhisattvas from whom Mahayana Buddhists seek help in their personal meditation.

Vajrayana meditation. Tibetan Buddhism developed an esoteric and intuition-oriented practice of meditation. They emphasize the guru-disciple relationship, stressing immediate and sudden enlightenment with the aid of *mandalas* (visual meditative aids) and *mantras* (repetitive words and phrases).

Zen meditation. Attempts to get beyond the good/evil conditioned duality of this existence through the use of *koans* or cryptic poems that carry the meditator beyond mundane logic.

Worship Times/Places

Since Buddha did not teach that gods are to be worshiped (because enlightenment is to be achieved by one's own discoveries), Buddhist meditative practices can take place anywhere. In practice, many Buddhists meet in temples and pay respects to Buddha images for inspiration in their spiritual journeys (and those of fellow Buddhists), but much meditation takes place in homes.

Food

Buddhists tend to follow Hindu eating practices, which means many are vegetarian. The emphasis is on eating foods that contribute to, rather than inhibit, spiritual practice. Thus, they encourage the eating of whole grains and fruits, foods that are easily and quickly digested and take as little energy as possible away from meditation. In some Buddhist countries, monks still beg for food from laypeople.

Gender, Marriage, Family

The Buddha granted women the right to become nuns (*bhikkhunis*), but he did so reluctantly. Given the patriarchal nature of India during his time, however, he was a socially liberating force.

American Versions

Zen. The most popular form of Buddhism in America. This individualized meditative practice came to America from Japan.

Nicheren Shoshu. A popular form of Buddhism in Japan,

Nicheren Shoshu is based on the teachings of a sixteenth century Japanese Buddhist saint who advocated regular chanting of the Lotus Sutra to bring health and prosperity.

Buddhist Vihara Society. The American version of conservative Theravada Buddhist meditative practice.

Tibetan. Concentrated in the Naropa Institute in Boulder, Colorado, a fully accredited four-year liberal arts college noted for its summer study programs.

Holidays

Major holidays center on the life events of the Buddha, his birth, enlightenment, and death. Sometimes they are celebrated on different days, sometimes one day. The most widely celebrated of these days is *Wesak*, observed sometime in May.

Common Misunderstandings

Nihilism. Buddhists are sometimes accused of being nihilistic because they view ultimate reality as being beyond the duality of the existence we all experience. The analysis is correct, but if nihilism is interpreted to mean uncaring, apathetic, or unethical, the charge is not true. Buddhist have devised nonultimate ethical teachings that apply to *samsaric*, this-worldly existence.

Self-centeredness. Buddhist practice, focused as it is on individual spiritual achievement, can seem self-centered. The later teachings of Mahayana Buddhism, particularly the bodhisattva ideal (a person capable of achieving Nirvana but who chooses to return to help others) does much to mitigate this impression.

The gods. Strictly speaking, Buddhists are atheistic; people must discover enlightenment themselves. The Buddha was certainly not a god. In practice, however, gods are recognized as able to help Buddhists in varying degrees by inspiring spiritual living, providing merit, and through occasional arranging of good fortune. In these roles, perhaps a more helpful (though still inadequate) Western equivalent would be saints or even guardian angels.

Current Relationships with Christianity

Historically the good relationships between Buddhists and Christians continue today. Perhaps one reason for this is the radical differences between the two religions. Another is the Buddhist's acceptance of and tolerance for those who believe differently than they.

Introductory Reading

Scriptures: Many volumes, including the Pali Tripitaka, Sanskrit Sutras, and Chinese, Japanese, and Tibetan translations, commentaries, and additions. A good anthology is edited by William Theodore de Bary, *The Buddhist Tradition in India, China, and Japan* (New York: Random House, 1972).

A basic introduction to Buddhism is Walpola Rahula, *What the Buddha Taught* (New York: Grove Press, 1974).

A popular periodical is the quarterly magazine *Tricycle: The Buddhist Review* (Address: TRI Box 3000, Denville, NJ 07834; Phone: 212 / 645-1143).

JUDAISM

Demographics

United States: 6,000,000. Worldwide: 14,000,000.

Key Dates

2000 B.C. Abraham migrates to Hebron and recognizes one God, Yahweh, as uniquely true and interested in his (extended) family's welfare.

1200 B.C. After years of slavery in Egypt, Moses leads the descendents of Abraham to freedom in Palestine.

586 B.C. Babylon fully conquers Palestine and takes the people of Judah into captivity in Babylon. Some of the Jews return to Palestine, but the land of Canaan is again occupied—first by Greece (331 B.C.) and then by Rome (63 B.C.).

70 A.D. After the Jews revolt, Rome destroys Jerusalem and scatters the Jews.

80–500 A.D. Deprived of a centralized temple and priesthood, the Jews develop a written Scripture and commentary to guide right living. The Babylonian Talmud was finished in this period.

1938 A.D. Centuries of persecution in Medieval Europe culminate in the Holocaust, in which millions of Jews are killed.

1948 A.D. Creation of the modern state of Israel.

Core Beliefs

Ethical monotheism. Belief in a single, personal, righteous God who is interested in the welfare and behavior of human beings.

Covenant. God selected the descendants of Abraham to be a chosen people, a vehicle of God's mighty acts in history.

Torah. For the Jew, his or her obligation to God is carried out through the observance of *mitzvot*—commandments or divine expectations that are of both a ritual (or particular) nature and an ethical (or universal) nature.

Land. Jews closely identify with Jerusalem and the land of Israel as a homeland promised by God.

Distinctive Practices

Prayer. One to three times daily.

Bar/Bat Mitzvah. Adult initiation ceremonies for thirteen-year-old boys and girls; the point at which Jewish young people become responsible for observing the commandments and divine expectations.

Worship Times/Places

Found in both synagogue/temple and at home. Sabbath begins at sundown Friday and lasts until sundown Saturday. Services are usually held both Friday evening and Saturday morning. Prayers, singing, reading from the Torah, and homilies on the readings are regular features of the service.

Food

Special dietary laws dictate for many Jews that they only eat *kosher* food; this refers to three things: (1) Allowable animal foods include sheep, cattle, goats, deer, fish with fins and scales, and certain fowl; (2) the slaughter of these animals must be painless and bloodless; all traces of blood must be removed from meat by soaking, salting, or broiling; (3) the combination of meat and milk is not allowed.

APPENDIX 2

Gender, Marriage, Family

Intermarriage between Jews and non-Jews is of great concern to the Jewish community. Recent statistics indicate that of all marriages in which at least one partner is Jewish, only 40 percent have both partners Jewish.

American Versions

Orthodox. Strict interpretation of Torah and kosher laws. No women rabbis. Approximately 10 percent of U. S. Jewish population.

Conservative. Torah authoritative, some kosher laws, some women rabbis. Approximately 32 percent of U.S. Jewish population.

Reform. Torah is to be adapted to modern times. Women rabbis. Approximately 23 percent of U. S. Jewish population.

Reconstructionist. Wide latitude in redefining Judaism for today.

Holidays

Passover. April-May (specific dates vary from year to year). This holiday celebrates the Exodus from Egypt under the leadership of Moses.

Pentecost. May. This holiday commemorates Moses getting the law on Mount Sinai.

New Year/Atonement. September. Eight high holy days of reflection, repentance, and celebration of *Rosh Hoshanna* (Jewish New Year).

Feast of Booths. September. Eight days of celebration of harvest and blessings. Families in temperate climate sometimes build "booths" outside and eat meals there to remember Israel's desert wanderings.

Lights. December. Also called *Hannukah,* this holiday is an eight-day celebration of the Jewish victory in the Maccabean war in second century B.C.

Common Misunderstandings

Christian extrapolations. Because Christians and Jews share a common history, Christians often view Jewish religious terms and teachings in light of Christian beliefs. The concepts often misunderstood this way include covenant, law, mercy, righteousness, messiah, salvation, heaven, and hell. It is best to ask Jews for their understanding of these teachings instead of assuming you already know.

Jesus. Jewish opinions of Jesus vary. Many accept him as a great teacher. As such he is not at all offensive to Jews, although they do not view him as the Messiah.

Current Relationships with Christianity

Anti-semitism has often characterized this relationship. We would like to think relationships are better today, and in some ways they are. On the other hand, acts of anti-semitism both in the United States (as documented by groups like the Anti-Defamation League) and elsewhere in the world are at an all-time high.

Jews do not think Christians are necessarily pagan. They tend to view peoples of other religions as capable of achieving salvation from the one, true God by following the provisions of the Noahic covenant in Genesis 9.

Introductory Reading

Scriptures: The Hebrew books of the Bible (what Christians call, to a Jew's chagrin, the Old Testament). See also the various, multivolume Talmuds—oral and written commentaries on the Hebrew Scriptures.

A basic introduction is Jacob Neusner's *An Introduction to Judaism: A Textbook and Reader* (Philadelphia: Westminster/John Knox, 1991).

Hundreds of Jewish journals are published. Interesting notes on world Jewry can be found in *The WJC Report*, published bimonthly by the World Jewish Congress (Address: 501 Madison Avenue, 17th floor, New York, NY 10022; Phone: 212 / 755-5770).

ISLAM

Demographics

United States: 4,000,000. Worldwide: 1,000,000,000.

APPENDIX 2

Key Dates

2000 B.C. Abraham and his son Ishmael, by Hagar, begin the family line.

571–629 A.D. Birth and death of Muhammad in Mecca.

629–661 A.D. Consolidation of extended Arabian penninsula by the first four rulers after Muhammad's death.

661–750 A.D. Rapid spread of Islam by Ummayyad Dynasty, across Northern Africa to Spain, north to present-day southern Russia, east to India.

750–1700 A.D. Rise and fall of Persian, Greek, and Egyptian dynasties, culminating in Turkish Ottoman Empire.

1700–1900 A.D. Dominance and then break-up of Ottoman Empire.

1900–1970 A.D. Western colonization and dominance.

1970–1992 A.D. Resurgence of Islamic nationalism, fueled by money from oil.

Core Beliefs

Monotheism. Strict reliance on one, personal, sovereign God, Allah.

Angels. Beings that live in the spiritual realm and do Allah's bidding.

Revelations. Principally the *Quran*, the book Allah revealed to Muhammad in oral installments. Allah has made 104 such revelations to human beings, four of which are extant: the Torah, the Psalms, the Gospel, and the Quran. Only the Quran, however, has remained uncorrupted by followers.

Prophets. Twenty-eight prophets are mentioned in the Quran, most of them biblical figures. Muhammad is the most important, the final messenger.

Judgment. All humanity will be judged at the end of time according to whether or not they submitted to Allah and his teaching in the Quran.

Distinctive Practices

The Five Pillars. These are practices that every Muslim follows: (1) recitation of the *shahada* ("There is no God but Allah, and Muhammad is Allah's prophet."); (2) prayer observed five times a day (dawn, noon, afternoon, sunset, bedtime); (3) fasting from dawn to dusk during the month of Ramadan; (4) almsgiving to the poor, widows, and orphans; (5) pilgrimage to Mecca at least once during the lifetime of every Muslim who is financially and physically able.

Missions. Dawah means Muslims are expected to spread the faith worldwide.

Law. Muslim law based on the Quran, the sayings of Muhammad, and oral traditions is called *shariya.* In countries where they are a majority of the population, Muslims believe the law of the land should be based on shariya law. Muslims do not distinguish between secular and sacred law.

Worship Times/Places

In addition to the five-times-a-day prayers, Muslims meet at noon on Friday at the mosque for community prayers. These prayers are the same as the daily prayers, but are done in concert. Friday prayers are often accompanied by readings from the Quran and by homilies on the readings.

Food

There are strong prohibitions against drinking alcoholic beverages and eating pork.

Gender, Marriage, Family

Women have well-prescribed roles in Islam. One of those roles is to worship separately from men at the mosque. In many countries women are restricted to household occupations. In some cultures polygamy is allowed. The Quran, however, says that before Allah women are spiritually equal to men. Men will rarely shake hands or otherwise touch a woman who is not his wife or child. A woman must not be left alone with a man who is not her husband. Muslims generally resist coed education when possible. Unchaperoned dating, coed gym classes, and coed swimming are prohibited.

American Versions

The traditional split in worldwide Islam is between *Shi'a* (10 percent) and *Sunni* (90 percent). American Muslims tend to downplay this distinction. In America a more common split is between mosques that insist on separation from "non-Muslim" aspects of American culture and those willing to do more accommodating—e.g., by using English instead of Arabic in some parts of prayer services, allowing coed learning situations, even reducing some dietary restrictions.

Black Muslims. Originally a non-orthodox, racist religion started by Elijah Muhammad in the inner cities of New York, Detroit, and Chicago, much of the movement now has embraced orthodox Islamic teachings.

Holidays

Hijra. July (Note: Muslims follow a lunar calendar, which means days rotate throughout Western calendar). New Year's day, celebrating the day Muhammad went from Mecca to Medina in 622 A.D.

Maulidan-Nabi. September. Birthday of Muhammad, celebrated by many Muslims.

Isra. February. Celebration of Muhammad's night flight to Jerusalem.

Ramadan. March-April. The month of fasting. This holiday includes *Leilat al-Qadr*, the night of prayer commemorating the Quran sent from Allah, and *Eid al-Fitr*, the joyous feast ending Ramadan.

Hajj. June. The seven-day trip to Mecca.

Eid Al-Adha. June. The feast of sacrifice, commemorating Abraham's great sacrifices.

Common Misunderstandings

Terrorism. Televised news from the Middle East has led some to the erroneous conclusion that all devout Muslims are in favor of terrorism.

Jihad. This word, meaning holy war, is interpreted variously by different Muslims. Only rarely has it meant conversion by the sword.

Current Relationships with Christianity

Politics often color this relationship more than with most other religions, in large measure because Muslims do not make the same distinctions between church and state that Western Christians do. Thus an act by a government of a country that has a majority

Christian population is seen by many Muslims as a Christian act, for good or for ill.

Introductory Reading

Scriptures: The *Quran.* Several good translations are available in inexpensive paperback. Many Muslims feel the one by Yusif Ali is best, though many other Muslims reject all translations.

A basic introduction is Thomas Lippman, *Understanding Islam* (New York: Mentor, 1990).

BAHAI

Demographics

United States 200,000. Worldwide: 4,500,000.

Key Dates

1819–1850. Life of the Bab, "The Gate," who in Persia in 1844 declares himself the one who will announce the Mahdi predicted in Islamic teaching. Thus, 1844 is the founding date of the Bahai faith. The Bab was executed in 1850, when he publicly withdrew from Islam.

1817–1892. Life of Bahaullah, the prophet-founder of Bahai, "The Glory of God" as the one promised by the Bab. He writes extensively on spiritual/political themes and is banished to Palestine in 1868.

1863. Bahaullah declared himself the "Glory of God."

1844–1922. Life of Abdul Baha, "Servant of the Glory of God." He travels extensively, spreading the teachings of his father Bahaullah.

1899–1957. Life of Shoghi Effendi, the grandson of Bahaullah. He leads the Bahai movment into the twentieth century.

1957. A new age in Bahai where leadership is not exercised by a single person but by a governing council. In the United States, the community is led by a nine-member National Spiritual Assembly.

APPENDIX 2

Core Beliefs

Oneness of God. God is everything. God's truth is a progressive, unfolding reality, and God sends messengers who represent successive stages in the spiritual evolution of humankind.

Oneness of Religion. All religions represent stages of the spiritual evolution of human beings. Each religious messenger has had an important message to increasingly wider segments of humankind: Abraham (tribe), Moses (people), Jesus (individual sanctity), Muhammad (nation), Bahaullah (collective sanctity).

Oneness of Humankind. We are all children of God, who should be working together to promote spiritual progress.

Distinctive Practices

No clergy.

Architecturally distinctive nine-sided Houses of Worship are located in Wilmette, Illinois; Frankfurt, Germany; Kampala, Uganda; Sidney, Australia; Panama City, Panama; New Delhi, India; Apia, Western Samoa; and Haifa, Israel (the world headquarters).

Currently they administer over 900 major social and economic development projects around the world, including medical centers, farming and fishing projects, and educational radio stations.

Worship Times/Places

Local meetings include devotional meetings, study groups, and social events. Their purpose is to know and worship God and to learn to carry forward an ever advancing human civilization.

Food

The Bahai faith prohibits alcohol and narcotics. An annual period of fasting is required, lasting from March 2–20, sunrise to sunset.

Gender, Marriage, Family

The equality of men and women is one of the main tenets of the Bahai teachings. They teach monogamy, promote chastity, and discourage divorce. Marriage is conditional on the consent of both parties and their parents.

American Versions

Administered by a nine-member National Spiritual Assembly, located in Wilmette, Illinois.

Holidays

The Bahai year begins on March 21 and consists of 19 months of 19 days each. The remaining four or five days are called intercalary days.

Naw-Ruz. March 21. New Year's Day.

Ridvan. April 21 to May 2. Twelve-day commemoration of Bahaullah's declaration that he was "The Glory of God."

Declaration of the Bab. May 23. Celebration of the Bab's 1844 declaration.

Ascension. May 29. Anniversary of the ascension (1892) of Bahaullah.

Martyrdom Day. July 9. Anniversary of the martyrdom of the Bab in 1850.

Birth of Bahaullah. November 12. Birthday of Bahaullah in 1817.

Ayyam-i-Ha. February 26 to March 1. The intercalary days devoted to festivities, gift giving, and charitable acts.

Common Misunderstandings

The mistaken idea that "anything goes" in Bahai is probably rooted in their acceptance of all religions. Bahais actually have a clearly defined religious program leading to human unity and world peace: fostering of good character, eradication of prejudices, dynamic coherence between the spiritual and practical requirements of life on earth, development of the unique talents and abilities of each individual, equality of men and women, advantages of a common world language, and universal education.

Current Relationships with Christianity

Bahais view Christianity and Christians as important players on the religious world scene.

Introductory Reading

Scriptures: The writings of Bahaullah, Abdul Baha, and Shoghi Effendi are very important. They also consider the various scriptures of the world's religions as important.

A good introduction is William Hatcher and J. Douglas Martin, *The Bahai Faith: The Emerging Global Religion* (San Francisco: Harper and Row, 1985).

The principle Bahai magazine is *World Order*, from the National Spiritual Assembly of the Bahais of the United States (Address: Wilmette, IL 60091; Phone: 708 / 869-9039).

NATIVE AMERICAN

Demographics

1,500,000 in United States. (Cf. approximately 1,000,000 in 1620 and approximately 300,000 in 1860).

Key Dates

60,000–8,000 B.C. Indian ancestors move across Bering Strait from Northern Asia and spread south through North America, Meso-America, and South America.

5,000 B.C. Indians establish agricultural communities in temperate and tropical zones.

Core Beliefs

Animal Ceremonialism. Native American religions see a close affinity between humans and animals; this manifests itself in imitation, rituals, and respect shown even when animals are killed for food.

World tree. For many tribes, a world tree ties the three dimensions of existence—heaven, earth, underworld—together in an almost permeable relationship, with freer interchange between the three realms than is the case with Western religions.

Spirits. There is usually a high God (e.g., the Lakota Wakan Tanka), but also many spirits on earth and in the underworld.

Distinctive Practices

Vision quest—an adult initiation ceremony. A young Indian spends two or three days in the wilderness, fasting and hoping for visitation by a spirit, usually of an animal. If successful, the animal spirit becomes the guardian spirit of the person.

Soul. Native American religions have a complex view of souls, parts of which are reincarnated, others parts of which go to heaven or the underworld. Many tribes believe souls remain with the tribe for one or two years.

Worship Times/Places

Rituals include purifications, feastings, and fastings. Purifications are often done in sweatlodges, smoking tobacco or anointing with smoke from sacred herbs. Special structures close to nature are often built for ceremonies.

Food

Traditionally they have tended to be subsistence cultures, either hunting or agricultural. Food patterns depend on seasonality and availability of food.

Gender, Marriage, Family

Gender and marriage laws vary along tribal lines. In some respects women play traditional roles in home and with children. On the other hand, in many Indian cultures the women have a strong voice in the selection of chiefs and leaders.

American Versions

There have been literally hundreds of Native American tribes, some still strong, others extinct. Religious practices, while having the common characteristics of a high god, interdependence, spirits, and animalism, can vary dramatically from tribe to tribe.

Holidays

Holidays vary from tribe to tribe, both in nature and time.

Common Misunderstandings

Spirits. Indians don't necessarily worship animal spirits or geographical spirits. They have great respect for all creation and the spirits that represent/permeate them, but most have a sense of a single great Mystery behind it all that demands our worship.

Current Relationships with Christianity

Relationships can be very ambivalent. In many tribes the old religious ways are threatened. Some Indians see this as a bad thing and are attempting to revive their traditional religions, sometimes in their pure form, other times by combining them with new forms of religion, such as Christianity.

Introductory Reading

Indian Scriptures are mostly oral. Some have been written down. A good collection is Frederick Turner, editor, *The Portable North American Indian Reader* (New York: Penguin, 1973).

The best single introduction is by Ake Hultkrantz, *The Religions of the American Indians* (Berkeley: University of California Press, 1967).

A good journal is *Akwesasne Notes: A Journal for Natural and Native People* (Address: P.O. Box 196, Rooseveltown, NY 13683).

CHURCH OF JESUS CHRIST OF LATTER DAY SAINTS (MORMONS)

Demographics

5,000,000 in the United States; 10,000,000 worldwide.

Key Dates

Pre-History. God is like us; he died and grew in wisdom, so that he became a celestial Father. We are his spirit children, with a plan of salvation that started with the creation described in Genesis.

Creation, Fall, Israel. Same as noted in Christianity.

721 B.C. The Assyrian exile with ten tribes of Israel forever assimilated.

600 B.C. Two distinct people groups left: Nephi and Laman fought.

421 A.D. Lamanites win; they begin the restoration of God's original plan of salvation.

1829 A.D. Joseph Smith receives the Book of Mormon and the power of the Aaronic priesthood lost at the Exile.

Core Beliefs

God. God is all powerful, single, but nontrinitarian and non-unique.

Salvation/atonement. Almost everyone will be saved and go to heaven because of the atoning death of Jesus Christ.

Eternal progression. Once in heaven, the saved continue to work for the spiritual progress both of those left on earth and of themselves; the final goal is exaltation, the chance to become head of a spiritual family ourselves, just as God is head of our spiritual family.

Priesthood. Two priesthoods—Melchizedek and Aaronic—for male members hold the only authority for ordination and baptism.

Distinctive Practices

Baptism for the dead. Baptism is essential. Those who missed it need it done by proxy. All worthy Mormons over twelve may be baptized for deceased non-Mormons. This is the reason for Mormon's extensive interest in genealogy; they want to baptize everyone possible.

Endowment. This is a special, secret ceremony in which individuals are given special knowledge, a new spiritual identity that enables them to continue to make spiritual progress in this life and the life to come.

Worship Times/Places

Mormons have several levels of meeting places: (1) Temples are holy sanctuaries where sacred ordinances and rites are performed. Salvation and activities required to enter the kingdom of God must be performed here. (2) Tabernacles are large meeting halls. (3) Wards are the equivalent of local churches. A geographical grouping of wards is called a stake.

Food

Mormons live by a fairly strict dietary code called the Code of Health. It proscribes wine, strong drink, tobacco, meats in the summertime, and all hot drinks. Recommended are all herbs, fruits in season, and wheat products.

Gender, Marriage, Family

Only men may enter into the priesthood. Intermarriage is forbidden. Two types of marriage are recognized: (1) regular, which may be done in the local ward and denotes permanent faithful bonding for this life; (2) celestial marriage or sealing, for all eternity, with the hope that the two partners will eventually be exalted and have spiritual children together.

Mormons emphasize family values and recommend that families have a family night together one night a week.

American Versions

Mormonism is a distinctly American religion, although Mormons are active in exporting it through aggressive missionary activity; all young Mormons are expected to donate up to two years of their life for missionary service.

There are two large branches of American Mormonism, both tracing their roots back to Founder Joseph Smith. The largest, the Church of Jesus Christ of Latter-Day Saints, is headquartered in Salt Lake City, Utah. The Reorganized Church of Latter-Day Saints is headquartered in Independence, Missouri (started in 1860).

Common Misunderstandings

Members of the Church of Jesus Christ of Latter-Day Saints do not like to be called a non-Christian religion, much less a sect or a cult. They consider themselves the true, restored church of Jesus Christ; salvation cannot take place outside the walls of the Mormon church.

Current Relationships with Christianity

Because they believe in the necessity of families to remain entirely inside the church, Mormons can come across as separatistic.

Some are, others are more open to interaction. Their basic religious exclusiveness, however, makes incidents of clashes with Christian groups fairly common, particularly in Western states and towns where they are in a majority.

Introductory Reading

Scriptures: Mormons read the Bible, but their central scripture is the *Book of Mormon.* Also important are two other books: *Doctrines and Covenants* and *The Pearl of Great Price.*

The best introductory volume is Jan Shipps, *Mormonism* (Chicago: University of Illinois Press, 1985).

The church's newspaper is called the *Deseret News* (Address: Deseret News Publishing Comany, Salt Lake City, UT 84130).

CHRISTIAN SCIENCE

Demographics

United States: 200,000.

Key Dates

1844–1875 A.D. Mary Baker Eddy has a series of life crises that develop her thinking: the death of her husband (1844); a failed second marriage; a search for physical healing with Phineas Quimby, who taught that disease was a thing of the mind not the body (1862); a severe physical accident (1866); and nine years of Scripture study (leading to the publication of *Science and Health With Key to the Scriptures* (1875).

1879 A.D. Mary Baker Eddy founds the Church of Christ, Scientist, in Boston, hereafter known as the Mother Church of the movement.

1895 A.D. Publication of the *Church Manual* by Mary Baker Eddy, giving directions for running Christian Science churches.

1910 A.D. Mary Baker Eddy dies at the age of 89.

Core Beliefs

Reality. The spiritual is more powerful (and in that sense more real) than the material. The Bible is not strictly speaking the story of

God working in history but of Jesus Christ showing us how to live a wholly spiritual life. This insight is the "key" to understanding the Scriptures.

Jesus. He is not divine but is the "key" or exemplar who has shown us how to overcome our misconceptions.

Evil. Evil is not real but may be overcome by yielding to the action of Divine Mind. Mortal mind accepts existence apart from God or Divine Mind. Overcoming this is tantamount to overcoming evil.

Salvation. Salvation is not just overcoming material evil, but great emphasis is placed on healing the wounds and scars, "physical" and spiritual. Tools include prayer, self-renunciation, and spiritual warfare.

Social Ethic. We must educate Christians to the need for healing worldwide. This is the function of the *Christian Science Monitor*, the movement's well-respected newpaper, founded in 1908.

Distinctive Practices

Church. Their religious organization is made up of 3,000 congregations governed by a five-member board of directors.

Reading Rooms. These are places to read daily readings in Eddy's *Key* and the Bible, as well as world news, all for the purpose of disciplined spiritual education.

Leadership. They have no clergy, no sacraments, few symbols, and no missionaries. Practitioners are full-time spiritual healers, charging fees on a basis similar to medical doctors. Lecturers are skilled in teaching about Mary Baker Eddy's writings. Individual congregations elect clerks to run the affairs of each church.

Worship Times/Places

Schedules similar to Christian churches. A typical worship includes silent prayer, testimonials, and daily readings.

Food

Christian Scientists forbid the use of alcohol, tobacco, and drugs.

American Versions

Christian Science is an American religion. There have been some splits from the main movement, but they are small.

Holidays

Traditional Christian and American holidays.

Gender, Marriage, Family

Many women are in leadership roles as practitioners and lecturers, following the founder's example.

Common Misunderstandings

Healing and the Law. Recent court cases of parents who have withheld medical attention from their children because of their belief in healing through spiritual power have brought attention to the movement. The cases have yet to produce a definitive legal position on whether parents have the right to withhold such care, or whether the state has the right to compel it. Complicating the cases are the fact that some states have explicit laws recognizing the priority of religious beliefs in this area.

Current Relationships with Christianity

Relationships are cordial, although the beliefs of Christian Scientists run so counter to traditional Christianity there can be no question of their non-orthodox status.

Introductory Readings

Scriptures: The *Bible.* Also, *Science and Faith with Key to the Scriptures, Church Manual,* and *Miscellaneous Writings,* all by Mary Baker Eddy.

A good introduction is Stephan Gottschalk, *The Emergence of Christian Science in American Religous Life* (Berkeley: University of California Press, 1973).

Christian Science Monitor (Address: The First Church of Christ Scientist, 107 Falmouth, Boston, MA 02115; Phone 617 / 450-2000).

UNITY SCHOOL OF CHRISTIANITY

Demographics

United States: Over 3,000,000 per year use the services of Unity.

Only a small percentage of that number (perhaps 60,000) are members of the church.

Key Dates

1886 A.D. Myrtle Fillmore is healed of a tubercular condition and declares, "I am a child of God and therefore do not inherit sickness."

1889 A.D. Charles and Myrtle Fillmore begin the Society of Silent Help and *Modern Thought* magazine.

1895 A.D. Charles and Myrtle Fillmore begin the Unity School of Christianity, with Charles as administrator and Myrtle as teacher.

1950 A.D. Unity Village, outside Kansas City, Missouri, is built.

1972 A.D. Charles R. Fillmore, grandson of Unity's founders, is appointed president.

Core Beliefs

Idealism. A modified idealism considers matter real and good, but it must be controlled by a right understanding and the use of the spiritual (ideal).

God. A spirit permeating everything. Because God is spirit, the Trinity is reinterpreted to mean Mind, Idea, and Expression.

Jesus. The ideal model of spiritual living; not divine.

Bible. The main textbook of Unity, but not the only one. The Bible is to be interpreted metaphysically, looking for the spiritual forms and realities behind the events and substances described in the text.

Salvation. Unity emphasizes practical, immediate salvation, not final salvation. Heaven and hell tend to be products of wrong thinking. Salvation is worked out over many lifetimes (reincarnation).

Path. Right thinking puts things right. Life can be directed by thinking and talking: (1) talk to your body, teaching it to respond; (2) have no negative thoughts; (3) seek forgiveness for misunderstandings.

Distinctive Practices

Prayer. Prayer is not talking to God, but creative thinking. Unity provides a prayer service for people called *Silent Unity.* People send prayer requests to Unity Village (7000 letters per day, 1800 phone calls per day). The requests are put in a tower called Silent Unity and are prayed for and answered in nine different languages.

Church. There are some Unity Churches (550 with about 60,000 members), but one can still belong to other Christian churches. Most people who use Unity belong to other Christian churches.

Education. Unity Village provides various educational experiences for training both clergy and lay people.

Worship Times/Places

Worship follows patterns of traditional Christian worship. The predominate feature is the constant, 24-hour-a-day phone counseling service.

Food

Vegetarianism is recommended. The kitchen at Unity Village is advertised as the world's most complete vegetarian cafeteria.

Gender, Marriage, Family

About half of all Unity ministers are women. Unity publishes the oldest children's magazine the the world, *Wee Wisdom,* founded in 1893.

American Versions

Unity is a made-in-America religion.

Holidays

No special holidays. Traditional Christian and American holidays.

Common Misunderstandings

As is evident by its name, Unity sees itself as thoroughly Christian. It does use the Bible as one of its scriptural authorities and uses Christian terminology throughout. But it so reinterprets Christian doctrines that it must be seen as something quite different from orthodox Christianity. Charles and Myrtle Fillmore saw themselves as rediscovering primitive Christianity, the real teachings of Jesus.

Current Relationships with Christianity

Unity does not see itself as a competitor with Christianity. Charles Fillmore often called Unity "practical Christianity."

Introductory Reading

For an insight into how Unity School of Christianity interprets the Bible, a look at *The Metaphysical Bible Dictionary* (Unity Village, Mo: Unity School of Christianity Press, 1959) is essential.

An introduction to the Fillmores is Hugh D'Andrade, *Charles Fillmore* (New York: Harper and Row, 1974).

The movement's periodical is *Unity* magazine (Address: Unity Village, MO 64065; Phone: 816 / 524-3550).

JEHOVAH'S WITNESSES

Demographics

United States: 800,000. Worldwide: 2,800,000.

Key Dates

1879 A.D. Charles Taze Russell, a Pittsburgh Presbyterian haberdasher, founds the Jehovah's Witnesses movement as the result of a Bible study group; he calls it Zion's Watch Tower.

1884 A.D. Russell begins the Watchtower Bible and Tract Society. He predicts the end of the age will come in 1914.

1916 A.D. Russell dies and is succeeded by Joseph Rutherford.

1942 A.D. Rutherford dies and is succeeded by Nathan Homer Knorr.

1977 A.D. Knorr dies and the church changes to a 14–18-member governing body rather than a single authoritarian leader. Current president of the governing body is Frederick Franz.

Core Beliefs

Bible. The Bible is to be interpreted literally by the Jehovah's Witnesses organization and not by individuals; they accept only the Jehovah's Witnesses official translation, the *New World Translation of the Holy Scriptures.*

Jehovah. The proper name of God, found over 6,000 times in the *New World Translation of the Holy Scriptures.*

Jesus. Jesus was not divine; there is no Trinity. Jesus was the first creation of Jehovah, a human life paid as a ransom for human beings. He died on a stake, not a cross. He was raised from the dead as a spirit and is present in the world today as a spirit.

End Times. The end is close and has already been predicted several times (1914, 1918, 1920, 1925, 1941, 1975). The date is figured variously: from the time of Adam in 4026 B.C. to 6,000 years later; or similarly, from the time of Eve; or from the length of the corridors of the Great Pyramid in Egypt, which Charles Russell viewed as a prophecy in stone. After missed dates, membership usually falls off, levels, and then begins to climb again.

Eternal Destiny. Evil people will be annihilated. Of the good people, 144,000 will be recreated to live with God in heaven, the rest to live with Jesus Christ on a recreated, paradisical earth.

Distinctive Practices

Proscriptions. Jehovah's Witnesses are allowed no images of Jehovah, no interfaith contact (including contact with Christians), no blood (in food or transfusions), no clergy or clergy titles, no pledges of allegiance to a flag, no birthday celebrations, no voting, and no service in armed forces.

Door-to-door mission. Public testimony is required, and careful records are kept of calls. It takes an average of 740 calls to make one convert to the Jehovah's Witnesses faith.

Publishing. The Watchtower in Brooklyn is an extensive publishing operation. Every Jehovah's Witness is expected to donate time to publishing by working at the publishing house as a volunteer or by selling subscriptions locally.

Neutralist. Because Satan rules this world, Jehovah's Witnesses do not serve in politics or armed forces. They are not pacifists, strictly speaking, but neutralists or separatists.

Worship Times/Places

Local assemblies are called Kingdom Halls (50,000 worldwide). Members meet on weekends and midweek for study and worship. Worship format consists of songs, Bible study, and prayer.

Food

Jehovah's Witnesses cannot eat food that contains blood.

Gender, Marriage, Family

Women cannot be elders or overseers in churches, but they do have a ministry to the public in witnessing and evangelism.

American Versions

Jehovah's Witnesses is an American religion. Because both Russell and Rutherford were strong willed, authoritarian men, splinter groups have been created. A few survive, including the Dawn Bible Students and the Layman's Home Missionary Movement.

Holidays

They do not celebrate Christmas, Easter, or Lent.

Periodically Jehovah's Witnesses call mass rallies. A recent one in New York's Yankee Stadium drew 250,000 people.

Once a year they hold Memorial (Holy Communion) on the biblical anniversary of Christ's death, the fourteenth day of the Jewish month of Nisan.

Common Misunderstandings

Because Jehovah's Witnesses believe taking blood into the body through the mouth or veins violates God's laws (based on Gen. 9:3; Lev. 17:14; Acts 15:28), they refuse blood transfusions even when life is threatened. This has led to some court cases involving minors for whom parents have refused transfusions.

Current Relationships with Christianity

Jehovah's Witnesses desire as little contact as possible with Christian groups. By and large, they are strict separatists.

Introductory Reading

Scripture: The *Bible,* only in the *New World Translation of the Holy Scriptures.*

A good introduction is Herbert Hewitt Stroup, *The Jehovah's Witnesses* (New York: Russell & Russell, 1967).

The movement's main periodical is a bimonthly with 10 million circulation, *The Watchtower* (Address: 25 Columbia Heights, Brooklyn, NY 11201; Phone: 718 / 625-3600).

UNIFICATION CHURCH

Demographics

United States: 30,000. Worldwide: 3,000,000.

Key Dates

1920 A.D. Birth of Sun Myung Moon.

1936 A.D. Moon has a vision in which Jesus asks him to help restore Christianity worldwide.

1954 A.D. Moon founds the Tong Il society in Korea—known in the U.S. as Holy Spirit Association for the Unification of World Christianity or the Unification Church. His followers are known as Moonies.

1970 A.D. Moon moves to the United States. Activities include lecture tours, conferences with academics and church leaders, business ventures (fishing, real estate, newspapers, ginseng trade), and establishment of theological education (a seminary in Tarrytown, New York).

1982 A.D. Moon is convicted on a tax evasion charge and sentenced to 18 months in prison.

Core Beliefs

God. God is a personal, all-powerful creator.

Creation. Adam and Eve were created to provide God with a living give-and-take relationship with creation, them, and their children.

Eden Plan. Adam and Eve would mature in the Garden of Eden to a state of spiritual perfection and then marry, and their children would populate a sinless world.

Fall. Before Adam and Eve had time to mature spiritually, Lucifer had a sexual (spiritual) relationship with Eve. Eve then persuaded Adam to have a physical sexual relationship. Thus, love became Lucifer-centered, not God-centered. This is original sin.

Restoration. Things could be set right only by a Messiah and his wife coming to earth and completing what Adam and Eve failed to do. These "True Parents" would then have sinless children.

Jesus. Jesus failed this mission of restoration. Much of the blame goes to John the Baptist, who failed to prepare the way properly. As a result, Jesus was murdered before he could marry and do his job.

Second Advent. A Messiah and his wife are still needed. Although Moon will not explicitly claim this title, most of his followers believe that he is the Lord of the Second Advent and that he and his wife have fulfilled this need.

Distinctive Practices

Indemnity. In order to pay God back for sin, we humans need to work long hard hours in his service—thus, the long hours Moonies work in witnessing and in the religion's businesses.

Pledge. Moonies commit themselves to that work, made the first of every week, month, year, and on holy days.

Conferences. Academics and politicians are particular targets for Unification Church trips and conferences. Groups of each will be brought together, often in exotic vacation retreats, for discussion of important world problems, usually ending with Moon's Unification answer.

Worship Times/Places

Sunday morning pledge services, with men on one side and women the other. The pledge is repeated in unison, in which the members recommit themselves to the Unification Church. A leader then prays for twenty minutes.

Food

Moonies always carry "holy salt" with them to sprinkle on their food to purify it. Smoking and drugs are banned.

Gender, Marriage, Family

Celibacy. A desired state before marriage and for sometime after marriage until conditions are right for consummation.

Mass marriages. Because the basic unit of humanity is a man and a woman (not individuals), the choosing of a marriage partner is extremely important. Moon does this and then performs weddings with hundreds of couples, some who have never met each other.

Communal living. Members live together in houses, often for the purpose of raising money for the Unification Church. Residents rise early, have a short worship service and inspiration for the day, and then go out for 14–16 hours to sell flowers or tea, or just to ask for donations.

Holidays

Periodic seven-day fasts are held, during which Moonies make special efforts to witness to as many people as possible.

American Versions

Because the movement is so tightly controlled by Moon, there is really only one version, his. He has basically combined a great deal of Christianity, Taoist dualism, Korean shamanism, and good business sense in order to create an efficient, profitable religion.

Common Misunderstandings

Because of Moon's wealth and high profile, we usually overestimate the size of the Moonies. At most, 30,000 belong in the United States (that is probably a generous estimate). The people attracted to the movement, however, are above average in intelligence and social standing, and are given first rate educations at Ivy League schools once they are members. This, when combined with Moon's personal contacts and influence, makes the small movement quite influential.

Current Relationships with Christianity

The Unification Church is very interested in good relationships with Christianity and other religions. One of their subsidiaries, International Religious Foundation, Inc., has sponsored a number of interfaith dialogues, and in 1985 held the First Assembly of the World's Religions in New Jersey.

Introductory Reading

Scriptures: *Divine Principle* is their official source. The Bible is also authoritative.

A good introduction is Eileen Barker, *The Making of a Moonie* (New York: Oxford, 1984).

Miscellaneous materials are available through their headquarters in the United States (Address: The Unification Church, 4 West 43rd Street, New York, NY 10036; Phone: 212 / 997-0050).

NEW AGE

Demographics

As many as 10,000,000 people in the United States use New Age books, medico-spiritual therapies, or psycho-technologies.

Key Dates

100 A.D. Development of gnosticism in Middle East.

1893 A.D. Swami Vivekananda travels to the United States from India to speak about Hinduism at the Chicago's World Fair; he effectively personifies Eastern religions to Christian America.

1920s A.D. Albert Einstein's theory of relativity does more than reform scientific thinking. It contributes to philosophical relativism, from which New Age thinking draws a great deal.

1960s A.D. A time of moral and spiritual revolution among the baby boom generation.

Core Beliefs

Monistic pantheism. New Agers believe God is not a kindly white-haired gentleman sitting in the sky, but that God is within every person—everyone is a part of God.

Relativism. Truth is neither absolute nor rational; religious truth is affective, a part of one's feelings. As such, it is personal and verifiable only by one's own judgments. No one's truth is wrong, yet no one's truth is necessarily true for anyone but himself or herself.

Intuition. Humans rely overmuch on rational thinking. There are many ways of knowing that go beyond the boundaries of the rational. People know through their own intuitions, through spirit contacts, and through ESP.

Self-help psychology. Since everyone is part of God, the answer to human problems lies deep within each person. All people must find techniques and technologies that will allow them to probe, purify, and perfect themselves.

Consumerism. The test of truth is neither orthodoxy (right thinking) nor orthopraxy (right doing); rather, the test of truth is whether it makes a person feel better and do better in his or her own personal spiritual quest. The religious customer is always right.

Distinctive Practices

Because any spiritual practice that works to achieve spiritual growth is good, New Age encompasses an extraordinary variety of ritual and worship. A few categories include:

Healing Therapies: Acupuncture, Acupressure, Aveda, Rolfing, Oil Baths, Reflexology, Aromatherapy, Massage, Colonic Massage

Spirit Contacts: Psychic Readings, Channeling, Clairvoyance

Psycho-technologies: Yoga, Meditation, Hypnotism, Psychometry

Energy Amulets: Crystals, Pyramids

Esoteric Hermeneutics: Numerology, Tarot, Astrology, Palmistry, Fung Shui, Graphology

Worship Times/Places

Variable

Food

Diet often plays a huge role in New Age thinking. The variety of diet is endless.

Gender, Marriage, Family

Since New Age is so individualistic, it is open to any and all. Gender and family thinking is not developed—it probably doesn't need to be, since the variety of practice would be wide indeed.

American Versions

A few of the possibilities include:
Arica Institute
A Course in Miracles
Erhard Training Seminars (e.s.t.)
Shirley MacClaine's writings
Urantia

Many movements have New Age elements, but would not properly be called New Age.

Holidays

Again, the variety is endless.

Common Misunderstandings

In some circles, to label something New Age is equivalent to saying it is modern and forward thinking. In other circles, such a label is equivalent to saying it is heretical. The truth is probably somewhere in between. Of course many New Age practices and beliefs run counter to orthodox Christian doctrine and must be rejected. But many have valid points in challenging ways Christians have needlessly restricted the all-encompassing truth of the Gospel. New Age teachings need to be evaluated on their merits, one by one.

Current Relationships with Christianity

The core beliefs of New Age are not compatible with orthodox Christianity.

Introductory Reading

Texts are legion.

Two good introductions to the movement are available. One is from an advocate: Marilyn Ferguson, *The Aquarian Conspiracy: Personal and Social Transformation in Our Time* (New York: St. Martin's Press, 1976); the other is from a critic: Russell Chandler, *Understanding the New Age* (Waco, Texas: Word Books, 1988).

There are many New Age periodicals on the market.

For Further Reading

Introduction

There are few good histories of Christian approaches to religious pluralism available. The first eight chapters of Paul Knitter's *No Other Name* (Maryknoll, NY: Orbis, 1985) are probably the best summary of how we have arrived at where we are today. Helpful also is the first chapter of Eric Sharpe's *Comparative Religion: A History* (Peru, IL: Open Court, 1986). My own *Alien Gods on American Turf* (Wheaton: Victor Books, 1990) traces the development of pluralism in America. Thomas Oden's *After Modernity, What?* (Grand Rapids: Zondervan, 1990) details implications of present pluralism for the future by calling us to the past. See also Diogenes Allen's *Christian Belief in a Postmodern World* (Louisville: Westminster/John Knox, 1989), John Cobb's *Christ in a Pluralistic Age* (Philadelphia: Westminster, 1985), William Placher's *Unapologetic Theology: A Christian Voice in a Pluralistic Conversation* (Louisville: Westminster/John Knox, 1989), and Lesslie Newbigin's *The Gospel in a Pluralistic Society* (Grand Rapids: Eerdmans, 1989) for discussion of other approaches to the issues of pluralism and Christian theology.

Chapter 1 The Religions Are Coming

Many authors have detailed the facts of growing religious pluralism. In addition to the books mentioned in this chapter, consider E. Allen Richardson's *East Comes West* (New York: Pilgrim, 1985). For information on specific religions in America's neighborhoods, more and more good resources are available in most libraries, including the *Encyclopedia of Religions*, edited by Mircea Eliade (New York: Macmillan, 1987), 16 vols.; the *Encyclopedia of the American Religious Experience*, edited by Charles Lippy and Peter Williamson (New York: Scribner, 1987); and the *Encyclopedia of American Religion*, 3d edition, edited by Gordon Melton (Detroit: Gale, 1989).

Chapter 2 Should I Fear the Challenge of These "New" Religions?

Robert Bellah and Frederick Greenspahn recently edited a collection of essays, *Uncivil Religion* (New York: Crossroad, 1987), a frank look at interreligious hostility in America. Greenspahn followed that book with another collection that he coedited with Martin Marty, *Pushing the Faith* (New York: Crossroad, 1988). It used to be that the crisis of pluralism was discussed in terms of Judeo-Christian denominationalism (Will Herberg, *Protestant, Catholic, Jew* [Garden City: Doubleday, 1955]), or the relationship between Christianity and culture (H. Richard Niebuhr's *Christ and Culture* [New York: Harper & Row, 1951]), or the struggle between church and state (Anson Phelps Stoke's *Church and State in the United States* [New York: Harper & Row, 1950]). The discussion still includes those things, but it must now also include the other religions. Recent works are Richard John Neuhaus's *The Naked Public Square* (Grand Rapids: Eerdmans, 1984), Charles Colson's *Kingdoms in Conflict* (Grand Rapids: Zondervan, 1987), and A. James Reichley's *Religion in American Public Life* (Washington, D. C.: Brookings, 1985). See also James D. G. Dunn's *Unity and Diversity in the New Testament* (Philadelphia: Westminster, 1977) for a discussion of pluralism in Scripture. Trends in the growth/decline of Christianity and the religions worldwide are described statistically in David Barrett's *World Christian Encyclopedia* (New York: Oxford Univ. Press, 1982).

Chapter 3 But Aren't the World Religions Trying to Take Over?

On the mission enterprises of other religions see the article on "Missions" in the *Encyclopedia of Religions.* Particularly helpful in seeing missions and Christianity through the eyes of non-Christians is Paul Griffith's *Christianity Through Non-Christian Eyes* (Maryknoll, NY: Orbis, 1990). Stephen Neill's *A History of Christian Missions* (Baltimore: Penguin, 1964) is still a wonderful summary, but David Bosch's *Transforming Mission: Paradigm Shifts in Theology of Mission* (Maryknoll, NY: Orbis, 1991) sets the context for today.

Chapter 4 Aren't All Religions Basically the Same Anyway?

There are classics representing the variety of answers to this question: Hendrick Kraemer's *The Christian Message in a Non-Christian World* (Grand Rapids: Kregel, 1938) still articulates the exclusivist position well. Karl Rahner in *Theological Investigations*, Volume 5 (New York: Seabury, 1966) was the principal inclusivist writer, but Gavin D'Costa's *Theology and Religious Pluralism* (Cambridge, MA: Basil Blackwell, 1986) furthers the inclusivist argument. John Hick's *An Interpretation of Religion* (New Haven: Yale Univ. Press, 1990) has become the standard pluralist text. The series *Faith Meets Faith* from Orbis Books usually champions the pluralist viewpoint but recognizes the other viewpoints in volumes like one that D'Costa edited, *Christian Uniqueness Reconsidered: The Myth of a Pluralistic Theology of Religion* (Maryknoll, NY: Orbis, 1990), a collection of essays by mostly exclusivist writers.

Chapter 5 If My Religion Is Right, Do I Really Need to Learn About Others?

There are many good introductions to world religions. A readable introduction is Huston Smith's *The World Religions* (San Francisco: Harper, 1990). A more detailed text is John and David Noss's *A History of the World's Religions* (New York: Macmillan, 1990). An evangelical approach to the study of world religions can be found in James Lewis and William Travis's *Religious Traditions of the World* (Grand Rapids: Zondervan, 1991). A shorter introduction from an evangelical viewpoint is Norman Anderson's *Christianity and the World Religions* (Downers Grove: Inter-Varsity, 1984). On the question of truth, see Hendrick Vroom's *Religions and the Truth* (Grand Rapids: Eerdmans, 1989) and Harold Netland's *Dissonant Voices* (Grand Rapids: Eerdmans, 1991).

Chapter 6 Doesn't the Bible Teach Us to Avoid Personal Contact with Non-Christians?

The Christian teaching on separation and secondary separation are useful for looking at this question. Check theological dictionaries and encyclopedias for further help.

Chapter 7 Should I Let My Children Play with Children from Families Who Believe in a Non-Christian Religion?

Denominational guidebooks have help for pastors on the questions of liturgical ceremonies such as marriage. For example, the Presbyterian Church (USA) Book of Order required that at least one of the partners in a marriage be a professing Christian (W-4.9002). Other denominational rules can provide similar information.

Chapter 8 Is It All Right to Worship with People of Other Faiths?

Most denominations have taken positions on this question. For example, the Roman Catholic Congregation of the Doctrine of the Faith, headed by Joseph Cardinal Ratzinger, published a document, "Letter to the Bishops of the Catholic Church on Some Aspects of Meditation" (Polyglot, 1989). In 1986 the Lutheran Church in America published a statement, "Interfaith Worship: Counsel for Lutherans." Check with your denomination for similar statements.

Chapter 9 Are My Non-Christian Neighbors Going to Hell?

Much of modern philosophy and theology would claim Friedrich Schleiermacher as father. See his *The Christian Faith* (Edinburgh: T. & T. Clark, 1989; orig. pub., 1821; English trans. 1928). Wilfred Cantwell Smith in *The Meaning and End of Religion* (New York: Mentor, 1962) brings universalism up to date. See also Hans Küng, *Theology for the Third Millennium* (Garden City: Doubleday, 1988). John Hick and Paul Knitter coedited a collection of essays, *The Myth of Christian Uniqueness* (Maryknoll, NY: Orbis, 1987), that offers the universalist and pluralist answers to this question. Clark Pinnock in *A Wideness in God's Mercy: The Finality of Jesus in a World of Religions* (Grand Rapids: Zondervan, 1992) and John Sanders in *No Other Name: An Investigation into the Destiny of the Unevangelized* (Grand Rapids: Eerdmans, 1992) offer different views of the evangelical inclusivist position. See also Mark Heim, *Is Christ the Only Way?* (Valley Forge: Judson, 1985). Bertrand Russell's *Why I Am Not a Christian* (New York: Simon and Schuster, 1957) is a good source of the naturalist position.

Chapter 10 How Should I Go About Sharing My Faith?

Discussion about motives can do no better than start with C. S. Lewis's *Screwtape Letters* (New York: Bantam, 1984) and Helmut Thielicke's *A Little Exercise for Young Theologians* (Grand Rapids: Eerdmans, 1962). On the various kinds of mission, see Robert Coleman's *The Master Plan of Evangelism* (Tappan, NJ: Revell, 1978), Bernard Ramm's *Varieties of Christian Apologetics* (Grand Rapids: Baker, 1962), and William R. Hutchison's *Errand to the World: American Protestant Thought and Foreign Missions* (Chicago: Univ. of Chicago Press, 1987). Francis M. DuBose has edited a good volume that includes some of the key documents of Christian missions, *Classics of Christian Missions* (Nashville: Broadman, 1979), and J. D. Douglas's editing of the documents of the Lausanne Congress on World Evangelism, *Let the World Hear His Voice* (Ashland, OR: World Wide, 1975) is helpful.

General Index

Scripture Index